THE WHEELS OF TRADE

DEVELOPING MARKETS FOR BUSINESS SERVICES

THE WHEELS OF TRADE

Developing markets for business services

MILENA HILEMAN AND JIM TANBURN

'Money . . . . is none of the
wheels of trade; it is the oil which
renders the motion of the wheels
more smooth and easy.'

David Hume

INTERMEDIATE TECHNOLOGY PUBLICATIONS 2000

Intermediate Technology Publications Ltd,
103–105 Southampton Row, London WC1B 4HH, UK

© Intermediate Technology Publications 2000

A CIP record for this book is available from the British Library

ISBN 1 85339 517 X

Typeset by J&L Composition Ltd, Filey, North Yorkshire
Printed in the UK by SRP, Exeter

Contents

5 EARLY EXPERIENCE IN MARKET DEVELOPMENT: INTRODUCING NEW SERVICES

Preface

POVERTY IS SYSTEMIC; those trapped in it are generally making very intelligent choices, and development aid is most effective when it harnesses that intelligence – rather than working in parallel with it. This book describes how that can be done, in the field of small enterprise development (SED).

Millions of poor people are involved in business activities, as they seek to work their way out of the poverty trap. Development workers have assumed for many years that incomes could be secured and enhanced by supporting those business activities, for example through training and counselling.

But rarely have interventions targeted existing providers of those support services, or Business Development Services (BDS). For-profit providers of BDS have either been assumed to be non-existent, or to be so hopelessly inadequate as to need wholesale replacement. The FIT Programme set out to be different, by building on and nurturing local initiative and creativity.

The FIT Programme started life in 1991 as an inter-regional project funded by the Government of the Netherlands, and implemented by the ILO and a Dutch NGO called TOOL. It has evolved over time, as other agencies have increasingly supported it, and unfortunately TOOL is no longer with us. But the Programme has retained its focus on learning how to work with the dynamics of the private sector itself.

Over the years, FIT has learned much about this, and the insights are captured in this book; they are related to specific examples and case studies drawn from around the world. The growing body of knowledge about BDS developed under the auspices of the Committee of Donor Agencies for Small Enterprise Development has been particularly helpful in this work.

We hope that all those involved in the development of small enterprises will find FIT's experiences stimulating and challenging. The approach which this book describes is substantially different to much of what is common practice today, in both attitude and practical details. It calls for constant reassessment of the assumptions underlying small enterprise development, and for substantial adaptation of current working methods, in order to get better results.

If this can be achieved, the approach holds the potential for reaching far greater numbers of people in need. The challenges posed by unemployment and under-employment were never as great as they are today, so the solutions contained in this book are particularly timely. We hope that you will join us in finding answers to the questions that still remain, and to realizing that potential.

Jim Tanburn
FIT Programme Co-ordinator
International Labour Office,
4 route des Morillons,
CH 1211, Geneva 22,
Switzerland

Acknowledgements

This book has been written primarily by Milena Hileman, Peter van Bussel and Jim Tanburn; Alan Gibson, Gavin Anderson and several others have made substantial contributions. It documents the work, in particular, of Jim Tanburn, Gavin Anderson, Tapera Muzira, Margaret Masbayi, Robert Nsiah, Margot Lobbezoo, Joseph Mathuva and Bert Wesselink. Nonetheless, many other people have also contributed to both the manuscript and the work itself, in various ways: thank you.

While many donor agencies now support the work of FIT, the seminal financing of the Government of the Netherlands is gratefully acknowledged. More recently, the Government of Austria, UNDP, the European Development Fund and Austrian OED have all contributed substantially. Similarly, while many people have contributed their energies and vision, the FIT Steering Committee has played a particularly important role in shaping its innovative character; their input is also gratefully acknowledged.

1. Introduction

MICRO AND SMALL ENTERPRISES span everything from the boy selling cigarettes on the street to the retired professor inventing a new technology. They include the small high-tech factory and the carpenter's shop that operates from a roadside stand. They provide services, sell international and local products, and very occasionally graduate into larger enterprises (many larger enterprises were once small). They help people survive when times are hard – and can offer independence and self-determined working hours and working conditions whether times are hard or not.

Research in Africa suggests they start up and fail most often when the economy is stagnating or slipping, and they expand to higher levels of productivity and small gains in employment when the economy is growing (Mead and Liedholm, 1998). They are certainly numerous, representing about a quarter of all working people in many countries, and 40 per cent of new entrants into the labour force in five countries in Africa that were surveyed (Mead, 1994). Government, large businesses, labour groups and associations, NGOs, training and research institutes, donors, and SEs themselves all have something to say, and plenty to do, to enable this 'sector' to develop positively.

However, the need for a new strategy for small enterprise development is increasingly clear. While more and more people rely on small enterprises for their livelihoods, very few of them have participated in development efforts that provide sustainable and effective business development services (BDS). Some progress has been made in the delivery of finance for enterprise development, yet the whole range of skills, networks, information and technical inputs that a well-developed market economy offers the aspiring entrepreneur are still inadequate or too expensive for most small business people in developing economies. Where services are available, social barriers or inadequate information may block access by poor, illiterate, or socially disadvantaged business people.

Until the 1990s, small enterprise development (SED) practitioners believed that state subsidized business development services should be provided directly to small business people. Thus, the state or charitable organizations provided training, technology, product development, business management skills and occasional support in marketing, on the grounds that the smallest businesses had neither the time nor the money to improve their operations. It is now believed that donor inputs may have distorted markets for business development services as much as they have strengthened them.

The potentially negative impact of donor- and government-financed service providers on the local market for BDS was recently reiterated in a paper summarizing real and virtual conferences on business development services for small and medium enterprises (SMEs):

> In many countries, the net effect of years of government and donor-supported interventions has been to undermine the development of market forces. Products delivered at low cost or free to SMEs induce a debilitating dependency and a cynicism over quality and value; providers offered easy and generous terms by donors develop a taste for these inflated fees which often bear little relation to real economy situations; they become motivated to pursue donors rather than, for example, private sector customers or sponsorship. Agencies have budgets that, above all, need to be spent – a predilection that may lead neither to considered actions nor to 'treading softly'. The result has been hugely distorted and largely dysfunctional markets, especially in low-income countries where institutions (including markets) are often more fragile and less able to resist the compelling pressures of hard donor money. Private sector BDS providers are, inexorably 'crowded out' (Gibson: 1999, p.4)

Lessons learned from micro-finance

Services sold according to consumer demand can and must be responsive to fluctuating markets and the changing requirements of small enterprise[1] (SE) customers in ways that services centrally planned and financed by projects, governments and NGOs may not. Thus, the alternative approach to direct provision of services to small business people is to enable the private sector to offer such services: the goal is now to find ways to facilitate transactions between private sector service providers and their small enterprise clients (Steel et al., 1999).

The micro-finance movement is partly responsible for this change. Rather than introduce foreign systems (such as formal banking systems), it finds

Box 1.1: Lira oil meeting fails over pay (*New Vision*, 19 November 1998)

Participants at a three-week course on oil extraction boycotted a closing ceremony on Friday after learning that they would not be paid allowance. Activities to end the course organised by Uganda Manufacturers Association and Northern Uganda Manufacturers Association came to a halt when participants locked themselves in a room shouting '*No money, no ceremony*' ... Attempts by officials to convince them to attend the ceremony were futile ... UMA Training Officer James Okweny said it was not UMA's policy to dish out allowances 'instead participants should pay commitment fees of about 30 000/- but we considered the people here are generally poor.'

2

ways to build on existing systems (such as peer pressure). In the case of BDS, explore the business networks, clustering patterns, or indigenous grassroots training and consulting that SEs commonly employ to develop their business. Alternatively, examine the market's spontaneous development of franchises for telecommunications services, or modify a common product to

Box 1.2: What are Business Development Services?

Traditionally, business development services refer to all non-financial activities set up by development agents to help small business people start or improve their businesses. The services include training, technology transfer, marketing, and business skills development. With private sector provision, the definition of business development services widens to any service that the market will bear. Thus business development services can support:

Production: access to tools and equipment, access to material inputs; facilitation/brokerage of linkages with suppliers and larger firms; organized SEs taking advantage of economies of scale in supply purchasing; technology dissemination; product research and development; information on competitor's products; importation services for supplies; vocational training; training in methods to reduce costs in production; clustering; advisory services; infrastructure; advocacy services

Marketing and distribution: identifying new markets; training on using customer feedback to develop new markets; providing information to meet standards and specifications of new markets; facilitating linkages to buyers; organizing SE producers to fill large orders; advertising services; market research services; export services; transportation services; communication services; advocacy services

Institutional Support: management and business skills development training; business tours; accounting services; secretarial support; developing management information systems; creating an entrepreneurial culture; standard setting; legal support; advocacy

Networks and Information: facilitating relationships among SEs and between SEs and larger firms; supporting the development of associations, clubs and professional societies; information services; messenger services; mentoring; advocacy

There are many different ways to classify services. According to the need or constraint they address, or the business activity to be addressed (see, for example, Goldmark, 1996). The important point is not what the service is, but how it functions in the marketplace – how it is, or could be delivered – and how it best can capture a particular market niche.

suit SEs, then license and support local manufacturers and retailers to sell it. Build on what is already there. Start with the local market for a given service, however imperfectly it operates, instead of replacing it with an externally financed alternative.

One possible difference, relative to micro-finance, may be that there were few qualms about the risks of 'crowding out' traditional money lenders.

Which small businesses are we talking about?

The focus here is on both the family-run and self-employed micro-scale businesses, and small businesses with fewer than 40 employees. This spans both the 'informal' business sector, for which survival is an achievement, and small businesses with higher growth potential. While this is a heterogeneous group as regards making investments to increase profits, the self-employed person simply surviving and the small business seeking to expand have much in common. With adequate information, both will make only investments that yield higher profits in the short term. The idea is not to encourage people to start businesses, for the evidence suggests that they need no encouragement. It is to focus on all viable, profitable businesses, whatever their size or degree of formality.

Defining an Innovative Approach: Developing Markets for BDS

The focus of the new paradigm is on developing markets for Business Development Services. Certain services (notably telecommunications and business and professional services) have an important effect on rapid economic growth and increased foreign investment.[2] An examination of how a service already functions in a particular market context becomes the starting point: the aim here is to focus on opportunities, rather than on needs, constraints or problems.

New questions are raised. What services do SEs believe warrant an investment of time or money? What services have they never had that might be useful? How can demand be met profitably? If demand is weak, why? What prevents service suppliers from meeting demand more effectively? What unique opportunities are there for mutual profit between smaller and larger enterprises? Answering these questions with the active participation of private sector service providers can lead to innovative and sustainable methods for meeting SE needs.

Interventions start by examining the present market operation, including the business networks and informal flows of information and technical assistance. People who have few social or material advantages are nevertheless able to make wise investment decisions, advocate for fair practices, and to be informed, discriminating consumers of services. As a local trainer from Fort Portal, Uganda, herself a small-scale entrepreneur and

Box 1.3: Which Markets?

When talking about markets for business development services, while in some cases one might wish to discuss larger market trends as they affect a particular region or country, in the following pages the reference is to very specific local markets – markets for service products that are embedded in larger social, political and economic contexts. This might mean the market for advertising, for example, or the market for export processing services. It could refer to something as large as the market for business management training, or as small as the market for exhibitions.

Put together all the markets for specific services and you have the markets for BDS. A well-developed BDS market offers services to all segments of the market – to the larger high-paying clients who can afford an expensive media campaign to introduce a new product, and also to the majority of micro-entrepreneurs who normally purchase only a sign for their shop but who might well benefit from setting up a stand at an exhibition in another town. The more services available – the more choices SEs have. The more competition between providers – the more likely the price and delivery system will match the pocketbook and preferences of SEs.

Up one more level to the entire market – the local economy, certain principles become important to facilitate the growth and expansion of specific markets for BDS. The assumption here is not that free markets are sufficient for economic growth and social prosperity, though they are considered necessary to a significant extent. Rather, it is that open vibrant markets offer opportunities for both micro- and larger enterprises to prosper, and for interdependencies, networks, and mutually beneficial relationships to grow. Market imperfections in developing countries tend to penalize smaller businesses. In an increasingly global economy, it is possible for interdependencies between smaller and larger firms to be mutually beneficial. Markets in the broadest sense of the word are the locus for identifying business opportunities.

a peanut-butter business, reports, the greatest demand may come from the poorest SEs, who look to services to make up for the education or social privileges they lack:

'If I am not sponsored [to conduct training] it is not a problem for me. SEs are willing to pay anyway, especially those who cannot read and write, because they realize much better that they need the course.

They are often the most eager to pay because they have not been allowed to take the training the NGOs offer, which require that you can at least read and write a little.'

'Mary', a for-profit SE trainer, 1999.

This innovative approach, to develop private markets for BDS, was given widespread publicity at the BDS Conferences of the Committee of Donor Agencies for SED, in Harare (1998) and Rio de Janeiro (1999); the proceedings of those conferences have been published separately (Levitsky, 2000 for the Rio conference). The shift in approach has so many implications for the delivery of development aid that many now refer to it as a shift in paradigm; the differences which it implies are summarized in Table 1.1, below.

The FIT Programme: Harnessing the Dynamism of the Private Sector

One of the key papers to propose this new paradigm in Rio described the FIT programme[3],which has tried to find ways to 'harness the energy and dynamism of the private sector'[5] to challenge the parallel provision of donor-funded services.

The 'emerging paradigm' captured at the Harare and Rio conferences largely matches the long-held vision of the FIT Programme. Perhaps it is more accurate to say that the FIT programme has helped to shape the new

Table 1.1:Developing markets for BDS: how is the approach different?[4]

	Traditional paradigm	New paradigm
Objective	• Provide quality services that SEs can afford	• Encourage others to provide quality services for which SEs are willing to pay
Starting point	• Diagnosis, of needs, surveys	• Knowledge of market (supply, demand, potential)
Point of Intervention	• First tier (direct provision or provision through a single local institution)	• Second tier (facilitate, regulate, develop service 'products', work with several providers, esp. in private sector)
Duration of Involvement	• Semi-permanent: donor-funded programmes must continue if services are to be available to SEs	• Temporary, with exit strategy: withdraw as markets develop
Subsidies	• Provided at the level of the service transaction • Justified on the basis that SEs cannot be expected to pay full costs	• More often provided at the level of the facilitator • Justified in the short run if market development impact outweighs market distortion impact; in the long run only for equity or public goods reasons (an open issue)

paradigm in so far as the programme is defined as a discrete entity. FIT has been a highly inclusive programme, bringing together a broad range of development practitioners and business people in Africa and around the world. If indeed a 'paradigm shift' is emerging, then all those who have helped the programme work toward its vision are part of this process.

The FIT programme's aim was to identify demand-driven services that could be financially sustainable or even profitable, i.e. low-cost and replicable for implementers, as well as relevant and useful for small business people. The first four years built the capacity of local NGOs and trade associations to organize their own BDS, facilitated as much as possible by private sector organizations. Today the programme adapts or develops services for local markets, but relies primarily on commercial providers for delivery.

FIT's experience suggests that not only are the poor willing to pay, but they will be better off if they do. As paying clients to providers who need their business, they are more likely to be in a position to influence local markets to serve their needs, or to generate further business opportunities. As recipients of free or subsidized services, they have little market power. Furthermore, those who offer services commercially need to be supported, not stifled, by public-sector investments.

> While we do not believe that all BDS can be provided commercially, we believe that it is absolutely imperative that those that can are clearly identified so that 'donor-propped' services do not destroy an existing or possible future, private service. We believe that the list of potentially commercial services is very wide. Where subsidy proves necessary to include certain sectors, then channelling these through existing private service providers will, at the least, avoid destroying the private market and may well strengthen it.
>
> G. Anderson, Manager, FIT Uganda

Developing BDS Markets for Equitable Economic Growth

The implicit goal of FIT and others is to support the creation of a market environment in developing countries where MSEs of all scales and types may find a wide range of affordable services to improve their businesses. The service providers depend on satisfying their discriminating SE customers to prosper. A market which offers a range and variety of business services targeted for all segments of clients is inherently good for all business and thus for economic growth. Economic growth is always part of the goal; equitable economic growth is a refinement of this overall goal. More transactions between businesses create the potential for information and linkages to flow at every level. A denser market for BDS products offers more opportunities for innovation or improvement in products, services, and business practices, and creates larger networks that can challenge monopolies or unfair practices.

7

SEs are an expanding market

Even today's 'most developed' markets may not offer services that inherently benefit smaller businesses. The most lucrative commercial services are likely to be targeted at larger businesses. Careful interventions can help the providers of business services to recognize the potential for profits by tailoring their products to the needs of smaller business. SEs are potentially a huge and growing market. Interventions using public funds are justified because SEs represent the majority of all business in many developing nations, and a substantial portion of all those who work at all. Analysis of the GEMINI surveys in five African countries[6] found that small enterprises absorbed nearly 40 per cent of new entrants to the labour force in a 10-year time period (1983-1993) (Mead, 1994).

Small businesses are often the only means of survival for people in countries where industrialization cannot keep pace with population growth. As firms downsize, parastatals privatize, and civil services are streamlined, the number of people starting new businesses is likely to increase. While the sector may not have the highest growth or job creation potential, increased opportunities to improve the smallest businesses can be expected to raise the standard of micro-enterprise performance, help foster larger and more vocal networks, and improve job quality across the board.

Would focussing on commercial services for larger enterprises be more effective?

The theory that smaller enterprises ideally graduate or grow into larger ones is no longer a strict orthodoxy. Multiple systems of production exist simultaneously, depending on the particular mix of resources, policies, and historical precedent. Today, evidence from around the world shows that small and large enterprises are complementary, each playing an important role in rapidly changing production systems. Under current conditions most SEs may never grow significantly, yet they still create jobs that alleviate poverty, often empower women, and develop business networks that may expand and improve the market position for many. Social issues, such as working conditions, child labour, and the empowerment of marginalized groups, could be addressed through services to SEs.

Where do small businesses fit in the global equation?

In a global economy, there is greater interdependency between businesses. From the smallest local producer to the transnational corporation – the need to adapt and innovate to suit changing circumstances is universal. Further,

> increasing consumer choice and access to knowledge and new means of communication have made individuals and social institutions not merely subjects but also potential actors in the process of globalization. Social

preferences influence market outcomes and have an impact on corporate reputations. A good corporate social image is increasingly essential for business success.[7]

Global communication has increased the power of the consumer, the press, and most elements of civil society. Corporate managers and politicians alike need to pay attention to the opinions and preferences of a larger and larger public audience. In this equation,

> SEs must be viewed, not as a marginalized group that requires ongoing assistance, but as one of the critical economic forces in developing countries. SEs form the majority of the workforce in many African countries. They are the major consumers in most African economies, purchasing raw materials, components, wholesale goods and services. Small business shops and informal traders perform the most effective retailing for many large and international companies . . . Many large companies view the small business as a critical and large potential market for services and products such as mobile phones, vehicles, and machinery, etc. This realization, combined with the fact that it is the fastest growing sector in Africa, indicates a growing and viable potential market for services, not a poor, marginalized group who are unable to articulate their needs, or understand their own business requirements. Once this realization has been understood the potential for commercial service development opens up.
>
> (FIT Uganda, 1999)

Win/Win opportunities

The need for transnational corporations to have a good public image brings many possible opportunities for creating services that benefit SEs, and SEs are important consumers and retailers for transnational corporations. Between the profit agenda of the commercial world, and the development agenda of government, donors, NGOs and others, lies an area that can be covered by both. By harnessing the private sector to address a development agenda, everyone – from the small business client to the business that is providing the service to the development agents who are trying to build an equitable society – is a winner. Profit motives and social objectives are, generally, perceived to be almost opposite. Yet, in the area of small enterprise development, the two can and should meet as often as possible. Recent experience of the FIT Programme in East and Southern Africa provides illustrative examples, based on a review of key documents and field visits to selected affiliate offices.[8] Examples of other efforts to provide win/win solutions to the challenge of creating effective and sustainable business development services are also presented based on a review of secondary sources.

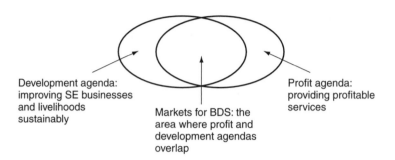

Figure 1.1: *Development and profit agendas can overlap*

This first chapter has established the main argument of the paper regarding small enterprise development and the larger economy. Chapter 2 presents a model for a new strategy to deliver business support services. Chapter 3 applies the model to one traditional BDS delivery system, a publicly funded business service centre. Chapter 4 introduces the FIT programme and presents its early experiences with service delivery through facilitator/providers, mostly NGOs, and offers more detail on the new approach advocated for service delivery. This is the background to the new paradigm for business development services. It also explains why the FIT programme has concluded that a local BDS facilitator actually needs to be a business, embedded in a local market and its own network of business relationships.

In Chapter 5, the latest experience of FIT and other SED programmes in Zimbabwe, Uganda and Kenya explore how new services can be introduced to markets sustainably, and how large businesses might be encouraged to mentor smaller ones in the context of a linkage contract. Chapter 6 presents ways to improve the outreach or quality of existing services in Paraguay and Eastern and Southern Africa. Chapter 7 suggests how impact might be measured by the various actors involved. Chapter 8 summarizes the conclusions of the paper. Before proceeding, some common definitions, outlined in the next chapter, are needed.

2. Setting the Terms of Discussion: A Model for the Delivery of BDS

THE PROFIT AGENDA aims to accumulate profits for the individual enterprise. Development agendas generally involve improving the 'health' of a large number of enterprises, often with a focus on smaller enterprises. The new paradigm for business development services occupies the area where the profit agenda and development agenda overlap, by seeking ways to develop markets for BDS products.

Thus, a new actor is involved, charged with finding ways to make a profit agenda aid and abet a social agenda profitably and sustainably. The diagram below shows the actors involved in project-funded micro- and small-scale business development services. It defines them according to their role, and illustrates whether the role is donor-financed or privately financed.

Actors and their roles

This chapter is devoted to outlining the model of intervention presented in Figure 2.1. Briefly, the individual roles may be outlined as follows:

Donors: Donors transfer public funds to achieve social or political aims. Donor funding is limited in time and by specific social objectives, which are monitored and measured.

International facilitators: The role of international facilitators is to develop new ideas, promote good practice and initiate innovation. Donors may play this role to some extent, but many are under pressure to reduce their staff. International facilitators can thus offer economies of scale in reporting, monitoring and evaluation, besides providing a neutral voice.

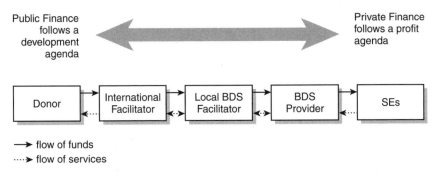

flow of funds
flow of services

Figure 2.1: *SED actors defined by functions and financing*

Local BDS facilitators: Local facilitators support for-profit BDS providers by developing new service products, opening new markets, setting standards, or advocating for favourable policies. They may also be involved in project design, monitoring and evaluation.

BDS providers: BDS providers offer business development services direct to SEs. They are the front-line players in the BDS market place.

SEs: The entrepreneurs who run small enterprises invest their time and money in business development services which they hope will increase incomes or secure survival.

The most significant element in this outline is the distinction between the local facilitator and the local provider. Traditionally, the donor-supported organization has often performed both functions, developing new and improved service 'products', and then delivering them too. Distinguishing between the two roles shows the potential for the local facilitator to support a wide range of independent local providers, instead.

Orientation: for whom do the actors perform?

Market players who receive the greater part of their income from public funds are placed on the left side of the diagram. In our model, these actors receive most of their finance from donors. Thus, almost all international facilitators and most local BDS facilitators are situated here – whether for profit or not for profit, they receive financing by convincing donors that they meet mutually defined objectives, on behalf of SEs. Since it may be import-ant to recover certain costs from the private sector to improve performance or establish transparent and effective relationships with their clients or bene-ficiaries, some of their income may also be derived from the private sector.

On the right side of the diagram are business development service providers who operate primarily in the private sector. They may sell services to small businesses direct, and meeting business needs generates most of their income.[9] Their performance is evaluated by private sector customers, who reward them with sales, contracts, or business deals. SEs also usually earn most of their income from the private sector, and so they too are on the right-hand side.

How are the actors' roles institutionalized?

Providers generally function more effectively when oriented toward small businesses, i.e. for profit, with income generated primarily from private financing. BDS providers on the right-hand side include private sector train-ers or training institutes, accounting firms, management consultants, master craftsmen, shops that provide communication services, advertising agencies, etc. and also a range of 'middlemen' who earn income by fostering business linkages. Under the new paradigm, publicly funded providers should not

12

crowd the private sector out of the market. Commercial provision should be helped to deliver more appropriate, cost-effective services.

A local facilitator could be a consulting firm, an NGO, an educational institution, an investment firm, a market research firm, or a project-specific organization. Local facilitators might develop new products, raise the standard of services, support service providers, and, in general, stimulate and support the market for BDS. With donor support they can take risks and incur relatively high costs to develop new products or new markets. However, by definition, a facilitator does not compete with, displace, or give a monopoly role to providers. If the same organization provides services to MSEs, or supports a closely linked provider, it takes on two separate and potentially conflicting roles.

In order to foster transactions that can be replicated by the private sector, the facilitator functions best when it behaves like a small business looking for ways to achieve profits, introduce new products, and identify investment opportunities. Its transactions with providers are on a business-to-business basis. To develop useful and practical products, and identify opportunities for profitable intervention, the BDS facilitator pays close attention to SE needs for business support, particularly to demand as measured by willingness to pay. At the same time, to secure and account for donor financing, the facilitator must pay equal attention to donor requirements and objectives.

Local facilitators: from business-like to being a business

The goal of the local facilitator is to improve the business development service market as a whole, and specifically to increase the range and type of services available to SEs. The facilitator helps the market to become more diverse, vibrant and competitive – so the market will offer useful and accessible business development services to as many small businesses as possible and practical. The facilitator may also help SEs become more discerning consumers of BDS products.

Investment capital from donors can easily distort a market, create a monopoly, or promote dependency. The local facilitator directs this capital to the private sector through business-to-business relationships with BDS providers. The facilitator points out ways that relatively small amounts of investment can create significant positive impact. In the process, the facilitator carefully monitors its own actions to avoid negative market distortion. In dialogue with donors and other public sector agencies, the facilitator is likely to play an advocacy role, so that basic policies and institutions necessary for small enterprise development are put in place.

How is the local facilitator different from other donor-funded organizations?

The local facilitator operates most effectively when it is structured as a small, streamlined, commercial business. It is not only seeking to further private sector development objectives – it has its own profit agenda. Because the facilitator is responsible for using donor funds to meet social objectives, the business needs checks and balances built into its structure. To ensure that a commercial agenda does not override a development agenda, contract payment can be linked to how well the development agenda is followed.

Commercial advantages: cost efficiency, networking, and staff incentives

It is preferable for the facilitator to be a commercial enterprise, since actually being a business keeps costs in line with the marketplace. In Zimbabwe, the market rate for a consultant might be US$ 25 day, for example, but six times that if a donor is thought to be paying the bill. A facilitator that is a business can be accepted as a member of the business community, and be taken seriously as a business partner, intending to remain in the market; donor-financed organizations tend to disappear. A facilitator will be looking for business deals or ways to charge BDS providers for the opportunities it identifies.

Operating as a commercial business helps the facilitator to stay in tune with the market for business development services, making it possible to monitor the market in general, and the market for specific BDS. Moreover, staff can be offered a new range of performance-related incentives. They could buy into the company, for example, or into a company with which the facilitator has a partnership. In the long run these incentives may be more attractive to staff than the short-term benefits of working for donors in organizations that come and go. A commercial company can institute reward systems that are logical and eventually offer some measure of security to its staff.

Relationships with donors

The decision-making structures of donors are complex and time-consuming; a facilitator operating as a commercial business can adopt a more dynamic stance by relating to donors as a business, specifically as a socially oriented investment or consulting firm seeking funding from donors on a contractual basis. Short-term contracts tied to specific outputs are a more effective means of financing activities than programmed core funding. Thus, funds are sought only for those activities that match its assessment of how markets for BDS can be stimulated or supported.

Facilitators need to inform donors of which activities require external investment in order to ensure the steady cash flow necessary to maintain a professional image in the business community. In a case in East Africa, a facilitator refused to undertake a number of SED consultancy studies for donors and chose to operate as an income–generating unit: donor funding for its planned activities had proved too unreliable. The problem facing the facilitator is how to supplement their donor contracts with business activities that do not compete with potential or actual providers, and allow them to operate professionally in the business community.

14

However, the facilitator's mandate prevents it from being purely a business: where activities appear too risky for a commercial provider, the facilitator can make use of donor funding. But a facilitator that needs to keep its eyes on the marketplace to survive is more likely to be in tune with the market than one that has adequate funding to cover all its activities. Indeed, FIT's experience is that too little funding is sometimes better than too much.

Motivation

The facilitator is motivated by its vision of what might be possible, in the immediate future, with small amounts of investment. Its role is to step in where it appears unviable for commercial providers, and demonstrate that development can result simply by direct sensible investment and by effective management of commercial enterprises, without the long-term patronage of foreign aid or government funding.

The role of the facilitator is also to find ways to combine the profit motivation of the business community with broader social concerns, creating win/win solutions. If the facilitator achieves this, it gains credibility in the business world and release from donor dependency. Thus, the facilitator is motivated by its flexible mandate to identify and demonstrate creative solutions and profitable opportunities that benefit SEs.

Local facilitators: what do they do?

As an organization, the facilitator will need to define clearly its development agenda and its vision. It will need a flexible business plan to determine its cash flow and financial prospects. It must constantly scan the marketplace for business support services, to identify opportunities where commercial providers could better serve SEs, and to respond to and monitor the results its own interventions. Its activities may also include the following.

Identifying opportunities

Unlike NGOs or projects, local facilitators do not depend on long-term work-plans. Whenever an opportunity is identified where development and profit agendas can overlap, they create short-term plans (from three months to a year) with clear exit strategies. As soon as possible, since opportunities depend on changing circumstances, the facilitator implements activities and evaluates results to incorporate into its next short-term plan. The activities usually involve test-marketing a service product in partnership with commercial actors.

Developing products

The relatively high cost of development of new services means that facilitators may take on the task of product development if they can find an investor to support the effort. The aim, in this case, is to lower the risk for privately financed BDS providers to try something new and untested.

Ultimate success comes when the private sector can innovate on its own, using whatever resources are available, to meet SE needs.

Opening new markets

The facilitator also has the task of proving to the private sector that a particular segment of the SE market, such as smaller SEs – often rural and run by women – are worth cultivating as clients for existing products.

Giving Voice to SEs and Advocating for Sound Policies

Advocacy, networking, encouraging linkages, awareness–raising and helping to create an enabling environment, are other activities that might be taken up by a facilitator. Viewing SEs as the clients of services, and SEs as important players in the market economy, is quite different from the traditional approach to small enterprise development.

Monitoring, Evaluating and International Support

Facilitators are responsible for using donor funds, and so may well provide the relatively expensive services of project design, monitoring of finances, activities and impact. The reporting needs to be in the language and style to which donors are accustomed. In this capacity they will benefit from the support of an international facilitator. Donor policy decisions usually take place on an international stage, and the international facilitator can also be a useful advocate.

Local facilitators are responsible for evaluating their own impact on the market. Ideally, the facilitator will be prepared to end an activity, or close down the organization, as soon as the private sector takes up the role of service provision competitively, making the services available to all levels of SEs that want them. In practice, the facilitator will want to find ways to sustain itself commercially. These tensions are explored further in subsequent chapters.

International facilitators: what do they do?

The international facilitator is closely involved in the process of developing local BDS markets; its functions include:

- *identification of good practice* and cutting-edge ideas globally, leading to the formulation of projects that are of interest to funding agencies, while also incorporating innovative approaches.
- *supervision*, so that local facilitators do not become exclusively profit oriented. This is particularly necessary where donors still operate formally according to a 'blueprint' approach; development of BDS markets requires a very flexible, 'process' approach. An international facilitator can reassure donors.
- *on-going support for local BDS facilitators* This comprises technical support (international expertise, contacts and ideas, etc.), and liaison with

donors at the international level. Innovative projects require much more support than traditional ones; local facilitators also benefit from encouragement and moral support. While regular visits are essential, far more can be done now by frequent e-mail exchanges.

- *cross-fertilization of ideas and lessons learned* As lessons are learned in one country, it is very important that they be disseminated to others; for example, if a publication is launched in one country information obtained about how newspapers are actually distributed may be invaluable for people starting a similar venture elsewhere. Similarly, liaison between local facilitators for exchange visits and study tours is important; experience has shown that active promotion and support is needed to establish an international network of local facilitators.
- *dissemination throughout the development community of lessons learned* This book is an example of one important function of an international facilitator: to disseminate lessons learned as widely as possible. Web sites, presentations in conferences, and other means are also necessary.

In the case of FIT, the international facilitator has been the ILO; there are a number of international NGOs that perform a similar function, but the same function could be performed by a for-profit agency, which could own shares in the local facilitators. This would have the advantage of maintaining some control over the local facilitators, and the directions they took in future. Indeed, local facilitators could also own shares in the international facilitator; however, as far as we know, this structure has not yet been put in place.

Why not direct funds to the private sector without a local BDS facilitator?

One might ask, why not fund the private sector direct, on condition that it develops and delivers the right sort of services to the right target group? Without the facilitator in between, the private sector provider is simply reoriented to a new client, the donor. The provider will no longer perform first for the small business market. Its donor income may create unfair competition. The facilitator therefore acts as a buffer, or filter, enabling the commercial sector to remain oriented toward profits that do not come from public sources of finance.

This vital function again highlights the need for the local BDS facilitator to look as much as possible like a local small enterprise. It should be operating with approximately the same financial scale and culture as small enterprises, or it will not perform its 'buffer' function. If an entrepreneurial BDS provider enters an office staffed by highly qualified people in suits, using expensive computers, the provider will quickly conclude that they may profit from an association with this organization, but not necessarily as an influential customer, buying facilitation services from a company oriented totally towards meeting their needs.

3. A Fresh Analysis of a Traditional Approach

The model applied to a business service centre

HOW DOES FIGURE 2.1 REALLY COMPARE with ongoing efforts to assist SEs? In many cases, the international or local facilitator creates an institution tailored to the objectives of donors and the needs of the target group, and offers services direct to the target SEs. For example, a business service centre might be established to provide training, advice, information, or help with establishing market linkages. Thus, our model would look like Figure 3.1.

The provider is offering training and counselling to SEs, but the provider is almost one with the facilitator who has established and supports it. The vertical line marks the public and private finance boundary. In our example, the goal is for the service centre to become a self-sustaining organization, financed entirely privately. Alternatively, a mix of private and public finance may be used, with recovery of some direct costs ensuring a productive transaction between provider and SE. In the example pictured, the centre is about 25 per cent privately financed. The rest comes from the local facilitator or from subsidies on SEs' payments for services. A number of actual centres operate thus, varying from 10 per cent private finance, up to 80 per cent.

Possible drawbacks of service delivery through a publicly financed centre

This approach presents a number of potential problems:

- Highly qualified and well-equipped staff mean costs may be high: profitability without public funds may be difficult.
- If profitability is pursued, the centres may have to target the high end of

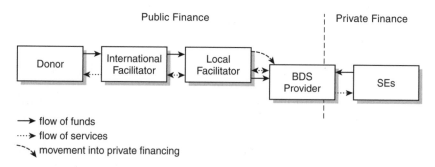

Figure 3.1: *Business Centre (mostly funded by the public sector)*

the market (prosperous SEs), and compete with private sector providers (not shown in Figure 3.1).

- If public funds are used, there is the possibility of losing the BDS focus in order to meet the objectives of the source of finance, as examples below illustrate.
- Isolation from the local business environment may make them less attractive to target clients.

Studies have found that when most of the financing derives from the public sector, costs are likely to be high (Goldmark, 1999). Often a service centre that covers all its direct costs is considered a success. The relatively high overheads (e.g. highly qualified staff) may not be calculated. Centres in Latin America that recover 30 to 60 per cent of their direct costs are considered successful, although in some cases 60 per cent recovery include subsidies paid by donors so that poorer SEs can use the services. Even those that have a profit goal consider 70 per cent recovery of direct costs after three years to be a significant achievement. Yet, running at a 30 per cent loss after three years, having received free technical assistance, would not be seen as such a great achievement by commercial standards. Sometimes the donor or international facilitator considers a centre to be self-financed if it manages to secure funds from other public sources, such as the government, NGOs, or other donors, although its position in the commercial market is virtually unchanged.

Dangers of not relying on market signals: trying to reach too many markets at once

The services offered by business centres range from entrepreneurship training for the SMEs most likely to succeed, to marketing SE products. Some centres suffer from trying to meet the needs of too many different SE clients. A study comparing a telecommunications franchise and a business centre set up by the local chamber of industries in the Philippines found that the smallest and least established SEs are mostly interested in lowering their transaction costs to maximize profits (Miehlbradt and Chua, 1999). More established SEs with higher incomes, have already learned how to reduce costs, and are in need of the specialized training or consultancy services that can help them expand their businesses.

Thus, providers should focus either on the transaction facilitator side of the service spectrum or on the enterprise skill development side: but not both. The authors recommend that business centres focus on the second group of clients, small in number but able to pay higher prices, rather than try to compete with the commercial franchise, which can more easily reach a broad spread of SEs. The commercial franchise was able to offer telecommunications services competitively, packaged in a way that appealed to SEs. (The same services were available at the same price from the national phone company, but without the comfort and service orientation of the commercial operation.)

According to the statistical surveys, only a minority of SEs have growth potential; thus, the common strategy of business centres with a profit goal to target the higher end of the SE market for services may be valid. But the assumption that the lower end is incapable of investment to improve their income, labour force or productivity means they remain unassisted.

Targeting SEs with high growth potential – is it effective?

Donor-funded business centres may be designed to serve only a limited number of SMEs with growth potential. In Uruguay, one programme reached 810 SMEs after 10 years, while in Brazil 10 000 were served; 10 000 appears significant, but it represents less than 1 per cent of the total SME population reported. Under a different programme in Indonesia, eight centres serve about 300 SMEs, and in the Philippines, eight centres serve about 420. This scale of outreach is not intended to make a significant impact on SEs. The selection process usually ensures that the few who are served are the true entrepreneurs: those most likely to succeed in business. This process makes it difficult to assess the impact of the business centre services on its clients, since these clients would be those most likely to succeed anyway. The majority's potential may be more modest, but their sheer numbers, particularly of new start-ups, may mean that their earnings support more people than the few highly successful small businesses.

The danger of crowding out the private sector

While business centres that are involved in retail marketing or creating business linkages have a good chance of profitability, they may also be competing with existing private providers; so may centres that target the higher end of SEs. Most centres offer some type of training or consultancy services, and these are often found in the private sector. Many centres report competition from consulting firms, universities, or non-profit providers, such as NGOs.

A Question of Style and Taste

Finally, a donor-funded service delivery system such as a business centre is not always the most suitable for SEs. As one observer at a recent BDS conference noted, one project in Africa 'built a very spacious business centre, a very beautiful building with all the computers, all the software, all the books and everything you need, located where the guys operate. But apparently the guys still are not coming. They aren't yet interested in the conventional ways of learning. They don't have a need for this kind of fancy building.'

Under what conditions do publicly funded business centres work best?

Where there are no privately financed providers – the Swisscontact Model

In some countries where BDS markets are very weak it is assumed that the introduction of a subsidized provider will encourage others to emerge. In cases where this may be true, Swisscontact offers a useful model for the provision of services through independent commercial business centres (see Hitchins; 1999). Donor funds are used to invest in a commercial establishment, with significant finance from local counterparts. Swisscontact, an international NGO, serves as the international facilitator, establishing a commercial partnership locally with the business centre provider.

All funding of the centre is tied contractually to financial performance and is offered on a declining basis. If income targets are not met, no monthly 'incentive' from Swisscontact is disbursed. The commercial partner can be any type of organization, including an NGO, as long as it operates the centre commercially and is selected by Swisscontact's tendering procedures. Experience suggests that partners with commercial backgrounds work best; this is consistent with lessons learned from the FIT programme.

Impact of subsidy and cost effectiveness

Since no other commercial consultant has access to the training and expertise that Swisscontact offers the business centres it sponsors, the centres are subsidized for only three years and must then compete without subsidy. But does the cost of monitoring and supporting the centres outweigh the benefits, given the relatively small number of SEs served? Close financial supervision by Swisscontact is necessary to disburse incentives to match targets, and such supervision is expensive.

Survival of the donor-funded centre need not be the main concern. Instead, the international facilitator could find ways to transfer ideas and skills to its competitors, or generally raise the level of service provision throughout the business counselling or training market. Even if the initial centre did not survive, if it developed different means of delivering the same types of services at various prices, it would be counted a success.

Economies in Transition: Three Business Centres from Romania

Some examples of weak BDS markets come from the former centrally planned economies. In Romania, for example, UNDP and UNIDO established a business centre in Bucharest in 1991, during the early stages of the country's transition to a market economy. At that time there were no commercial providers. The centre offered information, training, loan packaging and business planning assistance, and counselling. By 1994, it was evident that both the non-profit and the private sectors were competing with the centre, so funds were used instead to help local organizations start centres in smaller towns. Local sponsorship, either from the local government or the private sector, was required. Sixteen centres were established (three of which are reviewed in Kennedy et al., 1999).

Public finance preferred?

The choice of institutional arrangements was left to the local sponsors or partners, and few chose a commercial set-up. Perhaps because the centres were started with funding from UN agencies, the natural partners were public sector actors. Perhaps countries in transition from centrally planned economies do not see the logic of taking a commercial approach. This is unfortunate for the development of the BDS market in general. While most of the centres charge fees for their services, most of their income is from public sources, and their present activities reflect the demands of the donor clients. It is possible that in Romania the need for local development agencies to emerge to absorb the new influx of donor money may have been more obvious than the need for a network of commercial business centres. Businesses, after all, were finding some way, however inefficient, to meet their service needs, and donor financing was a newer concept. But when donor funds are paying for the staff salaries, rents and infrastructure, the services offered by the agencies are difficult to cost accurately. The input of donor funds is hard to separate out from the cost of services – staff and equipment are used for more than one set of activities.

Some centres are tied to local authorities and offer clearly subsidized services; others have evolved into regional development agencies, managing, for example, projects not directly related to small enterprise development. Those who have generated significant fees also moved their focus to larger businesses that can pay higher fees.

Losing focus, but even weak market signals are useful

Two of the three Romanian centres demonstrate the attractive force of donor funding, for two have become local development agents implementing a variety of donor-funded programmes, some of which have little to do with small enterprise development. The third centre shows the difficulty of maintaining an SE focus if there is no one acting as a facilitator, because it is much easier for a business to charge higher fees to the select few than low fees to the masses. SEs are a large and growing market, but a high-volume, low-margins market is not as instantly appealing to a small centre as one with low volume and high margins. Nevertheless, being 'business-like' and charging for services, is still useful to develop services that match market demand. For all three centres, initial income earned came from fees collected to help businesses apply for loans. Fees are now earned through specialized

Box 3.1: What constitutes an Entrepreneurial Approach?

Small businesses, particularly those run by entrepreneurs, operate in ways that are distinct from medium or large-scale businesses. Some of the characteristics of an entrepreneurial approach include:

- A high degree of responsibility for managers
- maintaining the freedom to experiment
- flexibility and a quick response time
- using intuition, learning by doing and by making mistakes.

Trusting managers to make independent decisions, coupled with access to small amounts of funding that is quickly disbursed, and the freedom to learn by doing (e.g. test-marketing services) has enabled FIT to adapt or change its objectives to meet market demands or take advantage of unexpected opportunities. Monitoring a dynamic work-plan and the way management decisions are made in response to client feedback and market realities is challenging.

Learning by doing, and by making mistakes, is productive if one can respond quickly. The programme constantly and rapidly assimilates lessons learned, and services and delivery systems are continually adapted or improved within the local BDS marketplace. Exchange visits become enterprise visits become business tours – FIT moves from funding NGOs to conducting pilots to offering tours through a joint venture to facilitating tours for all interested tour agencies.

Entrepreneurs constantly improve products or marketing strategies to keep up with the competition. For FIT, the specific outlines of a particular service product, and how it can best be delivered, are open-ended – improvement and adaptation to a particular market are dynamic and continuous processes. The search for innovative ideas and market niches are equally unbounded, but the ideas must be tested, developed and/or adapted in partnership with providers and their MSE clients. In this way, services will be relevant, affordable, profitable and replicable.

- seeking opportunities and networks

Seeking opportunities to expand or develop the area where the ethic of profit can intersect with a development agenda means placing a premium on innovation. Innovation is not sought for its own sake, but should be practical, building on what is already functioning in the marketplace, and finding ways to, for example, segment a market to reach smaller businesses. Looking at what works means examining the service and its delivery system in a specific market context. This systems perspective looks to the market to innovate and meet needs of MSEs profitably.

The FIT programme began with stakeholder consultations, primarily through focus groups and semi-structured interviews, and formal studies. Networks were formed and remain valuable, but today they include more businesses, and more businesses-to-business relationships.

- relying on feedback

Entrepreneurs seek customer feedback. A continuous process of stakeholder and client consultation remains central to the programme – to test and challenge new ideas, and to stay abreast of current events in the local economy and the market for business services. Studies, on the other hand, are now generally limited to market research, but with sufficient depth to satisfy donor interest.

Like many small businesses, the programme has been motivated by the vision and commitment of 'entrepreneurial' personalities associated with FIT from its onset. Their vision of development interventions that can harness the energy and resilience of the private sector to the benefit of the disadvantaged has been perceived as a minority view until very recently. Yet it has motivated individuals in the FIT network to work tirelessly, sometimes without any financial reward, in the search for practical ways to realize the vision, and to prove to sceptics that it can be done.

consulting services, because the days of easy low-interest loans have ended and the service is no longer in high demand.

Distorting markets?

The authors of the Romanian case study addressed the question of market distortion. They interviewed the few commercial counselling firms that had recently emerged in the towns where the centres were established. The firms said they do not face competition from the publicly financed centres. Commercial providers say they cater for different market niches or the higher-end of the SE clients. However, the centres may have inhibited the start up of commercial providers that would compete with the same segment of the market.

In the next chapter, the rationale for the new model of service delivery is explored further by examining the FIT programme's experience with delivering business development services through NGOs or NGO-like organizations.

4. The Evolution of the FIT Programme – An Entrepreneurial Approach

THE FIT PROGRAMME started in 1993 by taking an entrepreneurial approach to identifying new business development services in Kenya and Ghana. Some of the basic principles of good practice were axiomatic from the beginning, and remain guiding principles. Services should respond to SE demand, and be financially and socially sustainable. That is, they should be low cost and replicable for implementers, as well as relevant and useful for small business people. Private sector service delivery was encouraged, but the aim was to strengthen the capacity of local NGOs and SE associations to organize their own practical and sustainable BDS, in partnership with private sector actors.

Following the logic and lessons learned from the early years, and applying these to seven different country and programmes contexts, many elements of the programme changed and, over the past two years have approached a new paradigm for small enterprise development. Log frames have given way to flexible business plans. Targets like 'numbers of SEs that participate' are replaced by test marketing strategies. Most centrally, an entrepreneurial approach to business service delivery as well as service development has been institutionalized. This is because entrepreneurial aspects of the programme proved increasingly productive (see Box 4.1), and brought FIT to a model for programme development and implementation that takes on more and more of the modalities of small enterprises themselves.

There are many advantages to the new approach. Commercial facilitators and their for-profit providers are highly committed to the services they develop and market. Their enthusiasm, energy and ownership of interventions is unmatched by previous partners. The pace of implementation, especially of innovation and responsiveness to market conditions, is faster, richer, and more productive than in the early years of the programme. The potential for real sustainability and for reaching a significant scale of SEs is clear.

Flexible planning for short-term horizons is essential. Donors have little experience with funding commercial BDS facilitators, and do not necessarily understand how they operate. Facilitators are tempted to become providers, or to accept inadequate funds for their objectives, obliging them to find income-generating activities that do not conflict with their development agenda.

The idea of designing support service systems for SEs according to a private enterprise model is hardly new, but few BDS programmes have put the ideas fully into practice. As early as 1990, researchers and practitioners suggested that the best way to design service organizations for SMEs would be to model the organizations on SMEs themselves.

> More specifically, it has been suggested that the closer the support institution is to SSEs (small-scale enterprises) – in terms of the people, structures, behaviour and processes employed the greater the likelihood of a positive impact of services in catering to the recognised needs of entrepreneurs and in promoting a healthy development of the SSE sector. Conversely, the farther the support institution gets away from the enterprise model, the lesser the impact.
>
> (Gibb and Manu, 1990 p.22)

Nine years later, efforts to use a small enterprise model in developing or delivering BDS still appear young. The FIT programme had to learn, by doing, what sort of approach for service delivery could work. The older paradigm of at least partially subsidized service delivery through publicly financed organizations maintained a hold on some aspects of the programme until the birth of commercial facilitators. However, commercial BDS facilitators have been remarkably successful putting theory into practice.

First steps: following the logic of an entrepreneurial approach

An entrepreneurial approach to service development

During the first four years of the FIT programme, a number of business service products were developed and a strategy to generate customer-oriented and potentially profitable services emerged from pilot studies in Kenya and Ghana. Taking an entrepreneurial approach to the formulation of business services resulted in products that matched the SE markets in cost and content. Willingness to pay at least 50 per cent of direct costs was usually required. The approach is outlined in Box 4.1.

Product development relied on a process of sub-sector studies, test marketing (pilots) and mini-evaluations. Six service 'products' proved useful to SEs. For the successful pilots, local independent evaluations of participating SEs found they gained new products and technologies, new markets, new linkages and new ways of managing their businesses. In general, the successful services helped SEs become more market-oriented and customer-focussed.

The products do not require large investments of time or high levels of education from their users, and they can be offered inexpensively. Some were modelled on informal services that already function in the local market place, and others were local adaptations of services offered on a commercial basis in developed economies.[11] Pilot activities that were successful, were not dropped (e.g. capacity-building for SE associations and dissemination of

Box 4.1: Early Approach to Service Development

During the first four years, the FIT programme used the following approach to service development:

- starting from zero, FIT listened very closely to entrepreneurs, in order to discover exactly what they considered to be their constraints, and what types of BDS they might be willing to pay for in addressing those constraints
- starting points identified in this way were then developed through dialogue, drawing cautiously on ideas and experience in BDS provision by the for-profit private sector in other countries
- the services identified through this dialogue were then marketed on a pilot basis; initial offers were partially subsidized, on condition that the entrepreneur clients gave feedback on the design of the service
- the design of the service was then modified as quickly as possible in response to this feedback, so that it could conform more closely to what entrepreneurs wanted to pay for

(Tanburn: 1999)

Box 4.2: FIT Service Products

Through action research, in partnership with 10 implementing agencies in Kenya and 32 in Ghana, a number of support services and innovative delivery systems were developed under the first five years of the FIT programme. Further details can be found on the FIT CD-ROM. The service products include:

Enterprise Visits: Groups of entrepreneurs visit other large or small businesses. Visits sometimes take a training format, where host businesses demonstrate particular skills. Other learning takes place on a more informal level. The lessons learned cannot be predicted, as entrepreneurs pick and choose what seems most relevant to their own operations. Evaluations have found a considerable impact in all areas of business operation, including adoption of new technologies, management techniques and product lines. A manual on organizing and marketing exchange visits is available. Recently enterprise visits have evolved into business tours, where travel agencies arrange for SEs to visit a series of enterprises or other places of interest, such as trade shows.

Brokering workshops: While SEs can learn much by visiting other enterprises, they can also learn from each other in structured fora. Again, exchange of ideas, information and contacts can enhance all areas of business operation, especially when workshops are organized along sectoral lines, with maximum opportunities for exchange, and carefully selected technical input.

User-Led Innovation: SE producers are sometimes reluctant to enter into long discussions with the end-users of their products, as they expect some very negative comments, particularly in the area of product quality. Their customers, however, are often keen to participate. Once the criticisms have been aired, the SE producers find that they learn a considerable amount about customer demand for their products in terms of design, price/quality mix, availability, etc. A series of workshops, lasting three to six days in total, brings together producers and customers to modify existing or new products. Input from female customers has proved especially useful. A manual is available.

Sustainable access to information: SEs constantly seek information about markets, services, technologies and products. Often their main sources are family and local networks, which are not necessarily best placed to help them in their business. FIT has therefore developed a number of methods to disseminate commercially valuable information, from print media to radio.

SE Shows: SEs lack channels through which to market their products, especially to new customers. Experience has shown that SE exhibitions or shows, following the tradition of the agricultural shows, can help them to reach new markets. Furthermore, once SEs have seen the value of participating, they are keen to organize their own shows. A manual on organizing and marketing shows is available.

Rapid Market Appraisal: Many SEs adopt a rather passive approach to marketing. There is often an expectation that the customer should approach the producer, and not the opposite. A three- to five-day course brings producers together to 'brainstorm' on new product ideas, and to give them the 'tools' with which to interview potential customers. They then go out and interview those customers and key informants, returning to develop an action plan together. Evaluations show that the methodology does change SE attitudes towards marketing very effectively. A manual for trainers of entrepreneurs, and a manual for Training of Trainers (ToT), are both available.

designs for tools through photocopy shops). The programme also financed over 24 sector studies, and brought together a network of local small enterprise development agents, government representatives, and SEs in 10 national workshops or seminars.

Evolution of Delivery Systems

Delivery of Services through Donor-Financed Intermediaries

Initially the FIT programme relied on donor-financed organizations (mainly NGOs[12]) that functioned as both BDS facilitators and BDS providers to help develop and deliver services. Eighteen implementing partners were involved in two countries. As facilitators, they assisted with monitoring, product development, and testing and disseminating the products. They were the convenient channel for service delivery because they could access a readily available target group, demonstrate the potential for cost recovery, and plug into what was perceived as a grassroots network or 'community' of SEs. It was hoped that the service would be replicated by the organization and would help it become sustainable. Thus the model looked like Figure 4.1.

In Figure 4.1, fees from SEs contribute only slightly to the costs of the organization, most income being derived from donors, as indicated by the position of the organization box, just crossing the line separating public and private funding. The potential or actual commercial provider is missing from the diagram, because they do not exist or are inaccessible. For FIT-supported interventions developed during 1993-1997, FIT paid the design costs of the services, some of the overheads, and often 50 per cent of the direct costs. SEs paid the rest of the direct costs. The partner organizations paid the remainder of the overheads.

A Question of Scale

There were no immediately obvious problems with delivery using this model. NGOs delivered services well in both countries, while SE associations in Ghana performed better than those in Kenya. Although the interventions looked useful and sustainability – direct costs were covered by at least 50 per cent, and often more – it became clear that the pilots were not widely

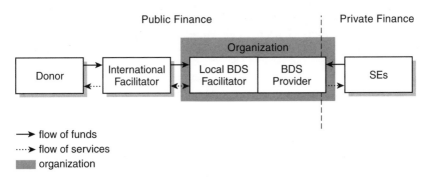

→ flow of funds
····► flow of services
▮ organization

Figure 4.1: *Service delivery through a publicly financed facilitator/provider*

replicated. In Kenya, three of the collaborating agencies went on to implement pilot activities on their own, and a number of others may have copied the same ideas; in Ghana, there was no evidence of continuation. At most, about 1000 SEs participated in one or more of the pilot activities. Because delivery on a large scale was not achieved, closer attention was brought to the question of how to deliver services sustainably.

As more effort was put into finding ways to encourage NGOs to be business-like, or to facilitate commercial service delivery, other limitations became apparent. FIT encountered the following obstacles in delivering services though organizations that operated as both facilitators and providers:

- NGOs often feel that a business-like approach is inherently exploitative.
- Some NGOs assumed that donor funding was a necessary precondition for continuation of the services
- Operating costs of service provision were often relatively high, and this limited the scale of outreach. A ceiling was soon reached, either in terms of cost, or the ability of the organization to cope with higher numbers of SEs.
- Supporting a single provider potentially discouraged competition from the private sector. It was hoped that NGOs would be able to demonstrate to SEs services that SEs themselves could then offer to their colleagues, and while a few cases of this was noted, in general SEs expected NGOs to continue offering services.
- SE customers knew that the organizations received external funds and offered substantial benefits to staff. Thus they expected benefits to be shared, and did not readily accept paying for services.

The birth of local BDS facilitators: market distortion becomes more apparent

To address such problems posed by delivery through publicly funded organizations, such as determining which services were in demand, local BDS facilitators were offered the opportunity of finding ways to collaborate with commercial providers. It was hoped that BDS facilitators would eventually become commercial providers themselves. However, it became clear that subsidized services discouraged the private sector from offering the services commercially.

In the early FIT years, when NGOs offered training in Rapid Market Appraisal or User-Led Innovation, consultant trainers who normally work for donors were employed because they had worked in the area of small enterprise development for a long time. The idea that there might be small-scale local trainers in nearby towns and villages employed by SEs without an intermediary was not even considered. Recent experience in providing or facilitating service delivery commercially has highlighted exactly how donor-funded projects can distort the local market for services.

Box 4.3: Meat-eating feast makes unfair competition, but local trainer prevails

Dorcas, who lives near Fort Portal, Uganda, had trained for NGOs in the past, but she never thought of making it a full-time business. Normally she waited for an NGO to contact her and ask her to conduct a course. When she saw an advertisement in the national paper offering a trainer-of-trainers course in Rapid Market Appraisal, she thought about marketing her skills directly to the SEs and sent off her letter of application. After attending the course, she was convinced that she had something worthwhile to offer her new clients, and she began trying to market herself by talking to SEs in her area. She had invested US$40 in the course and was very eager to try out her new skills and recover her investment.

Marketing the first RMA course did not prove easy. A government-sponsored NGO had recently organized training for SEs that was completely free and culminated in a party with free drinks and roasted meat. SEs asked her why they should pay her for training when others offered these incentives. Dorcas explained to the SEs that she was a business person like themselves, and just as they cannot offer free products to their customers, neither could she. This line of reasoning made sense to her clients and helped them identify with her. Finally she had enough clients to hold the first training (each paid approximately US$8). They responded enthusiastically to the training and, through word of mouth, the next session was much easier to organize. The SEs reported that one of the reasons they preferred Dorcas' training was because she trained in their local language, making learning easier and more enjoyable.

In many countries NGOs are under great pressure to become sustainable, and are pushed to compete with commercial providers, taking advantage of whatever comparative advantages they may have. For example, a review of the literature on BDS in 1997 concluded that private voluntary organizations (PVOs) involved in marketing for SEs can play a useful role when 'providing indirect, facilitative, or catalytic support, rather than attempting to operate as direct service providers. For PVOs to provide services directly to SEs, they will have to act and perform very much like commercial suppliers. In fact, to compete on a sustainable basis, they may need to establish such services as for-profit, commercial operations' (Barton, 1997). This statement probably holds true for almost all service provision, not only marketing. As FIT facilitators realized they would have to use commercial providers in most cases in the long term, the advantages became more apparent.

The assumption that commercial agents are inherently exploitative or hopelessly inadequate, and NGOs are inherently good, is not likely to be correct in the case of business development services. Without paying attention to the impact of subsidized services on the overall market for business development services, even the most carefully executed project might have a negative impact in the long term.

Commercial Providers Have Certain Advantages

Experience over the last two years of the FIT programme suggests that delivering services through commercial providers, with the mediation of a local facilitator, offers the following benefits:

- Competition can be encouraged and the dangers of creating a monopoly or discouraging new providers more easily avoided.
- Services cost less, as overheads are in line with the market served – the SEs. Freelance consultants who earn fees from NGOs and donors cost much more per day than SEs can afford. Recent surveys in Kenya, Uganda and Zimbabwe found that local trainers price their training to fit the market (the trainers were found to earn about as much as local teachers), and may even offer prices for the poorest based on ability to pay.
- SEs see the logic of paying the full costs of the services provided, and thus select only the services they value most.
- For those services that prove profitable there is the potential to replicate provision to a degree where BDS could reach a high proportion of MSEs in a given market.
- Service provision is highly flexible, allowing the design of the BDS to be adjusted rapidly in response to market demand instead of project cycles.
- Services are more likely to be embedded in local social networks and are thus more relevant and accessible. People who are part of the local market place also can offer continuous advice and access to an approachable business network. Local providers will be subject to social sanctions if they do not deliver the service expected with the impact envisioned.

Potential downside: a question of quality and the issue of exploitation

Commercial service providers may fall down on quality. Subsidized services funded by public sources can ensure delivery by professionals, and thus a high quality of service. However, it might be more productive to see how a service can be improved by assisting or challenging the existing providers to upgrade their services, or to raise awareness among SEs so that they can place pressure on the providers to deliver a better quality service, at an affordable price.

Does delivering services commercially subject poor business people to manipulation by their wealthier or more powerful colleagues? While the ethics of profit certainly do not preclude exploitation, adequate competition and consumer awareness can place a check on it. Successful businesses operating in a competitive market seek customer satisfaction. Customer satisfaction is achieved only by the provision of a useful and valuable service.

Address the root causes of poor quality or unfair practices

Concerns expressed about quality of services and exploitation by providers both suggest that SEs are not discriminating customers, but are both ignorant and powerless. It might be more constructive, and less condescending, to assume that SEs have the ability to become discriminating customers, to demand quality services, and to advocate for fair business practices. Clearly, more marginalized owners of SEs are as capable as anyone of making sound decisions, provided they have adequate information and opportunity to do so. Creating a parallel world of services for deserving SEs, where prices of services are low, quality is high, and practices are fair, will not necessarily address the root causes of the problems; instead it may mask them. In the parallel universe of subsidized services, SEs become dependent on an artificially-financed world, and the private-sector market for services has no incentive to compete and improve.

The Evolution of Local BDS Facilitators

Independent facilitators were created in a number of countries just when the major programme funding was drawing to a close. The way the facilitator is established and structured, and the role it plays, appear to be a very important part of how to capture the dynamism of market forces.

Establishing facilitators: seven examples suggest being a business works best

The experience of FIT-affiliated offices as they established more business-like organizational structures reiterates the need for a functional separation between facilitators and providers. It also suggests that being a business is better than being business-like, while being a visibly donor-funded organization can be counter productive.

In 1997, FIT offices in four countries used the lessons learned in the project to develop their own independent organizations to facilitate, develop, or deliver services. Few restrictions were imposed. Technical advice from the international facilitator (the ILO) and access to FIT service products were included in the package, but the offices could not claim to be linked in any way with the ILO. In some cases, very limited funds for start-up were offered, on a short-term contractual basis. FIT-affiliated offices in Uganda, Ghana, and Kenya all took on the challenge; Zimbabwe followed the same model, with funding from the Austrian Government, and three FIT sub-projects (in Tanzania, Benin and the Gambia) were set up under ongoing ILO activities.

Five offices had difficulties

Five of the country offices (Ghana, Kenya, the Gambia, Tanzania, and Benin) had a history of working closely and visibly with an international organization. They were associated with 'FIT the ILO programme', or another ILO co-sponsored project. These five had difficulty establishing viable relationships with the private sector.

In Ghana and Kenya managers have had trouble shaking off their ILO association, or changing their orientation away from donors and toward MSEs. Most of their energy was absorbed trying, with limited success, to secure donor funds. They were, thus, more oriented towards donor requirements than to the actual needs of the market, and consequently failed to innovate greatly.

The Gambia, Tanzania and Benin offices highlight the difficulties of initiating a market-oriented approach within the parameters of an ongoing donor-funded project. In two cases bureaucratic obstacles led to little movement of funds and no significant activities after a full year. It took implementors over a year to understand how to conduct FIT activities with the private sector. When they did begin collaborating, results were positive and commercial providers continued offering FIT services after the project closed.

Commercial, independent facilitators were the most innovative

In Zimbabwe and Uganda, FIT worked through for-profit facilitators, with neither the history nor staff of an ongoing donor-funded project. These two affiliates have been the most productive and innovative, offering valuable lessons for the others. The Zimbabwe affiliate was first housed in a project office. It was difficult to undertake any activities successfully until they moved.

> Things started opening up once I was out of the shadow of the project office. People stopped expecting free things and I was more accepted by the small guys and able to discuss issues. They can relate to me because I am also running a business.
>
> Tapera Muzira, Manager FIT Zimbabwe

Lessons learned from the first Commercial Facilitator

FIT Uganda was the first office to set itself up as a commercial operation, with the initial intention of being a provider. It soon recognized, however, that this role could easily compromise development objectives. Even when providing services through the structure of a joint venture, it became clear that the market was highly competitive, and giving support to a particular development service for SEs could take second priority to earning profits. FIT Zimbabwe went through a similar learning process, benefiting in part from the lessons learned by FIT Uganda. Each office has since seen that

Table 4.1: FIT Uganda: Objectives and rationale – then and now

Then Provider (1997)	*Now Facilitator (1999)*
To establish a profitable company through private sector income: • because this reflected the donor's interests to become sustainable • because of the belief that it would be more efficient and effective	**To develop the market for BDS for SEs** • because it is more appropriate and effective to support BDS providers who operate in the SE market • to avoid unfair competition **To develop a profitable company from all sources of income** • to be sustainable • to be independent, avoid being donor-driven • to maintain the identity of an equal partner in the business community • to motivate staff
To establish and support the establishment of BDS by providing BDS commercially, in-house or with partners through joint ventures • to get an income • to build on the previous experiences of FIT in developing low-cost and useful services • to gain experience, and credibility in the market	**To support existing and new BDS providers to develop or improve services to SEs** • so that customer-oriented services are available on a sustainable basis at affordable prices • so that externally funded activities have a clear exit strategy and the danger of negative distortion is minimized
To undertake consultancy services for donors • because banks were unwilling to offer finance • because donors were interested in FIT's agenda	**To identify financial and technical support activities and to undertake pilot activities to develop and introduce new BDS with donor support** • because experience suggests this approach offers the best hope for scale, customer-orientation, and sustainability • because consultancies can distract staff from their main objectives **To scan constantly the BDS market, provision and demand to identify:** • existing providers • gaps in the market (services and providers) **To advocate against negative market distortions created by publicly funded service provision and lobby for private sector delivery of services**

facilitating was more important than providing and has, therefore, shifted strategy. Table 4.1 outlines FIT Uganda's change in strategy from provider to facilitator.

How a commercial local facilitator finds opportunities to develop markets

Once it became apparent that the role of provider meant competing with the very commercial providers one would like to see strengthened, it also became clear that there might be far more effective ways of working, over a short time-span, to induce the private sector to offer services that help SEs improve their businesses. In the next chapter many of the case studies illustrate the kinds of questions facilitators must ask themselves before introducing a relatively new service to the market place, or upgrading services already offered commercially to SEs.

What is the rationale for intervening in a specific market for BDS?

Ideally the facilitator has identified a business opportunity it believes can benefit both SEs and commercial providers. It has found a space within the market where the profit agenda and the development agenda could overlap. How are these opportunities identified?

All the FIT examples built on previous BDS product development experience. The research, which included focus groups, sub-sector and other studies, and pilot tests of potential services, was assumed to be applicable to new countries. It was also useful to see what was available to small businesses in developed economies and to consider how the service could be offered in a local market. FIT managers took a trip to the UK to gain new ideas from for-profit BDS providers in the UK. *Business Connect* in Zimbabwe was inspired by the many commercial publications in industrial countries. Small business radio shows are also common phenomena in developed economies. Opportunities can be found from almost any source. Market research, networking, brainstorming, and constant dialogue with small and large businesses have all helped FIT facilitators find ideas that could prove to be opportunities.

The market is narrowed down to an opportunity

The overall goal is market development. To avoid distortion and damage to private BDS provision, selected activities around specific opportunities are planned. Once a potential opportunity is identified, the facilitator quickly undertakes focussed market research, using surveys, focus groups, and test marketing.[13] Market research is confined to one representative urban area, or one representative rural area, for example. The research method used depends on the nature of the product. Test marketing may provide surprising information and should be undertaken as soon as possible (Chapter 7 contains more details on surveys).

36

Table 4.2: Identifying opportunities in the market for BDS

Service Status	Likely Interventions
Service does not exist (e.g. commercial business tours, business-to-business advertising paper)	Develop service product in-house, pilot test, demonstrate viability to providers (e.g. though joint venture, business deals, licensing, etc.) provide service on short-term basis to encourage competitors
Service not used by SEs (e.g. commercial advertising)	Assist providers with service product development for SE market segment, pilot test with providers, special introductory offers, marketing campaigns
Service is of low quality (e.g. some training)	Service product development, advocacy, provider networking, establishing standards or regulatory bodies, introduce better quality to challenge providers, consumer awareness campaigns,
Service has poor outreach (e.g. advertising or some training)	Partnerships with providers to open new markets, consumer awareness, promoting linkages between existing and potential providers.
Service offered informally or inexpensively and functions well (e.g. commercial telephone and fax shops)[14]	No intervention. Monitor to develop models for use in new markets or with different products

Local market features determine how the service may best be developed. The gaps or opportunities present in the market place for support services will help determine what type of business relationship the facilitator should establish with providers – what type of entry point, and exit strategy, are appropriate.

Where commercial partners are involved in service product development, they always enter the partnership without being offered cash incentives. They are expected to contribute to the investment costs of product development, or even cover most costs, as for the radio station in Uganda.

Establishing a Commercial Local BDS Facilitator: Guidelines for International Facilitators

How does an international facilitator set up a local BDS facilitator who can identify ways to stimulate the market to provide services that can benefit SEs? The following guidelines are drawn from the suggestions and experience of FIT local and international facilitators. Essentially, the goal is to

37

establish a development office that takes a commercial and entrepreneurial approach to the development of BDS markets.

Before you go: establish a flexible funding mechanism

FIT's experience shows that funding is required by a local facilitator's office for at least one to three years, but should not be tied to a fixed time-frame or large disbursements. Funds should be disbursed to the facilitator by short-term contracts covering expenses tied to specific outputs. Successful completion of the contract earns final payment.

TIP The facilitator needs the freedom to learn by doing, but will operate most successfully if it needs to develop the business skills required to be able to finance itself. The goal is not to become a provider, however, and profitable interventions need an exit strategy.

When you get there: Orientation and overview

In order to guide and monitor your facilitator, learn as much as possible about the local market for business development services, without holding fast to any opinions formed. Information-gathering should not yet lead to strategic planning for specific activities.

Desk Study Assuming your normal duties have not already prepared you, begin with a desk study before arrival for an overview of the social, economic, and business environment in your chosen destination. Be careful: the FIT programme found certain assumptions widely held by development workers about their given SE sectors to be quite inaccurate.

Fieldwork The goals are to:

- gain understanding of the various business networks that operate, and the sorts of services that are available for medium, small or even microbusinesses
- identify a commercial facilitator (or possibly identify directors interested in establishing one)
- obtain knowledge necessary to establish an office – where to advertise, in which newspaper to place an advertisement for a manager?; what salary scale and benefits?; what regulations and requirements apply to a foreign investor who wants to set up a local firm?; how much does it cost to rent an office, pay for electricity?, buy a computer?

TIP First and lasting impressions are made early: business people will want to know your reasons for talking to them. The aim is not to be perceived as a donor representative searching for a way to disburse funds, but instead as a business person looking for investment opportunities that will benefit SEs. Make contacts and gather information through personal charm, rather than the status of belonging to an international organization.

Box 4.4: Sample Recruitment Advertisement

Foreign Investor Seeks Local Representative

A foreign investor seeks opportunities in the commercial provision of services to small business throughout Zimbabwe. These services may include helping business to reach new markets (for example, by organizing shows and exhibitions); access information (for example, through the media); find training; or to make contact with other businesses (for example through tailor-made package tours). A local representative is therefore being recruited to establish and operate an office in Harare. The representative will be responsible for identifying a range of viable services. He/she will prepare these services to the point where they can be test-marketed on a pilot basis. He/she will also identify possible commercial partners to collaborate with.

Qualifications: The applicant should have a relevant University degree and a proven track record of success in the business sector. Computer skills (particularly in the use of Internet) are essential. The post, which will be initially for one year, may also require some travel abroad, and an attractive package of remuneration is offered. The post is to be filled as soon as possible. Please apply with full curriculum vitae (including references). Applications must arrive by Friday, 6 February, latest.

Entering the Local Market

Recruiting and hiring a manager

Recruitment can be a long process. Place an advertisement in the most respected newspaper as soon as you arrive. Box 4.4 is a sample of the advertisement used in Zimbabwe.

In this example, candidates were shortlisted and invited to attend the first round selection process, bringing details in writing of the strategy they would employ to start up a business meeting the objectives of the foreign investor described in the advertisement. The top three candidates were interviewed again, references checked, and the manager hired.

Strategic planning

Strategic planning will clarify the overall vision of the company – what the local facilitator would like to achieve within two to five years. Use brainstorming and other creative techniques. Consider hiring a workshop facilitator or management consultant for a one-day event. Start with the vision, and move on to operational and administrative strategies. Establish the outlines necessary for a business plan. Hire someone to write down and type up all the ideas generated and conclusions made, leaving participants free to devote all their attention to the workshop.

TIP After the planning exercise, the manager may be somewhat bewildered. He or she needs to understand why the development objectives are important and why commercial objectives are equally important. He or she has to understand who the foreign investor is (initially a donor), and why this investor needs to keep a low profile. Visits to or from other local BDS facilitators are very helpful here. Allow the implications of the strategic plan to sink in before starting the six-month work plan.

Six-month work plan

The strategic plan sets the stage for a six-month work plan and budget agreed between you and your local manager. This forms the content of the manager's first contract, which should include terms of reference with specific outputs. At the end of the period, the facilitator should be ready to prepare a flexible business plan.

The major task of the six-month work plan is to orientate the manager to the market for business development services so he or she can begin to identify gaps and opportunities that can benefit small businesses. For local facilitators, market research is best undertaken by jumping straight into the market to develop a service product. At the same time, you need to decide whether you, the facilitator, or an external consultant, should cover the baseline monitoring necessary for programme development and future impact assessment.

The launch

More systematic market research is required, focusing on the needs of SEs and larger businesses. Instead of launching a major research exercise, however, experience suggests that a more modest study is best, followed rapidly by test-marketing of new services (for providers and/or SEs themselves). Focus groups can provide a very economical means to generate ideas, and to gain some understanding of the local market. Normal baseline study is expensive and rarely provides reliable indications of demand for innovative services, or even the actual willingness to pay.

Thus, the best away to identify real market opportunities is to 'ride on the back of one proven product', even if the proof comes from another country. The best product choice will allow the facilitator to learn as much about the SEs and the marketplace for business development services as possible. No more than two should be considered initially. None should involve subsidized services. For example:[15]

- *Business tours*: at first glance this is a good choice because designing and test-marketing the product will give the manager a great deal of information about the commercial interests of small business and will provide a good overview of the whole commercial sector. It also needs only a computer and energetic people to get it started – investment costs are low.

- *Business-to-business advertising paper*: although setting up this activity gives a good overview of the market, it requires relatively high investment and needs a good reputation to attract adverts. Too high a risk for a first activity.
- *Innovative training such as rapid market appraisal or user-led innovation for private sector trainers*: perhaps too specific a service. You are not likely to learn about the whole market but only about training because the SEs involved may be in too many different sub-sectors.
- *Radio Show for SEs*: developing the product entails networking with SEs and large business – will give a good overview of the market. The show will give visibility to the facilitator's company and help secure a professional image. Little investment is required, and the risk is low. A good choice to start.

The research, test piloting, test marketing, and monitoring methods will vary, depending on the type of service to be offered. First-year activities may establish valuable services, but they are also intended to teach the local facilitator how to take a dynamic entrepreneurial approach based on local market demand, rather than on donor preferences.

Develop a flexible business plan

Writing a flexible, minimalist, business plan, which outlines the possibilities and viability of the facilitator's activities, is an excellent tool to develop a business idea into a tangible business. The plan describes the purpose of the business and includes a description and analysis of the market, as well as the strategy, capacity, financial forecast and development schedule.

Estimating the need, cost, value, benefits and willingness of donors and local BDS providers to pay for the development of new and unknown services in the long run is hard to estimate. Much will depend on the results of the initial start-up and consolidation period of the company and thus on the availability of a flexible funding mechanism over the first period, the capabilities of the management and staff, and the support provided by the international facilitator.

Checks and Balances on the Business of Facilitation: A Proposal for the Future

Where there is no international facilitator to support a local facilitator, what alternative structure might take its place? The FIT programme undertook some research to see what kind of institutional arrangements could both support and help to manage a number of local facilitators.

Figure 4.2: *Relationship between International and National Facilitators*

One model has the international facilitator holding a majority stake in each local facilitator company; the international facilitator would be responsible for ensuring maintenance of the development agenda. Donor funds are channelled through the international facilitator, which disburses them via short-term output-oriented contracts. The owners of the international facilitator would have a background in development, and function as trustees for the organization. Potential dividends would be redirected toward the activities designed to achieve the overall objectives of the company. Normally they function only as monitors of financial activities and outputs, and offer limited technical support, unless there are enough funds to warrant more. Figure 4.2 outlines the model proposed.

Under this arrangement, the international facilitator might own 51 per cent of each of the affiliates. Of the 49 per cent of remaining shares, 5 per cent could be allocated to founding staff (to promote their motivation and loyalty), and the rest retained for future allocation, as appropriate. In addition, local facilitators could own shares in the international facilitator, if that had a for-profit constitution. Alternatively, it might be registered as a company limited by guarantee, in which case it would have only trustees, rather than shareholders or owners.

A draft Code of Operation for Local Facilitators is presented at the end of this chapter as Box 4.5.

Next Steps: The Way Forward

Where to seek finance?

Commercial local facilitators have no shortage of ideas after only two years of operations. The main difficulty arises from the change in relations with the donor offices, that are unused to working on the terms and conditions that have proved to function best; they may be eager to provide funds, once they see the results, but neither flexibly nor in the small quantities required. As one manager put it:

Our work highlighted that our ideas and approaches are problematic to donor procedures and involve considerable work for donor representatives. An NGO project that is non-profit, implemented under one partner, can specify numbers of MSEs to be supported (because it is not market driven but is provided almost free) and can specify their long-term strategy and approach, rather than being flexible according to demand or opportunity – this takes up little time or explanation, fits perfectly into a log frame and avoids complex issues of private sector exploitation. In short, donor funding has proven time-consuming and, because we are not being donor-driven (in fact we end up trying to educate donors), relatively unproductive.

Some FIT local facilitators have responded by establishing an income-generating activity, which raises their standing in the local business community. But finding a profitable activity that also helps the facilitator in its overall mission is challenging.

In the following chapter a number of the interventions undertaken by FIT Uganda and FIT Zimbabwe are outlined. Each of these activities builds on the knowledge gained in the FIT programme in Ghana and Kenya, but instead of simply orienting activities around what was planned and learned, the facilitator looks to the market to find commercial partners to deliver the services.

Box 4.5: Code of operation for Local Facilitators

International Facilitator Ltd. is a holding company for three facilitator companies with a social objective to promote enterprise through the development and provision of high-quality business development services.

Each local facilitator company abides by a code of operation to ensure that both the company's social and profit objectives are achieved.

1) *Company Focus*

- Local facilitator companies aim to demonstrate private sector solutions to development problems and will not invest in, support or establish any service that is not deemed, by the International Facilitator Ltd. board, to be promoting business development.
- At least 70 per cent of each company's staff time and financial resources will be channelled into researching, establishing and developing BDS aimed predominantly at the micro- and small enterprise sector.
- Local facilitator companies will utilize donor funds only to innovate and experiment in service delivery and, where possible, promote and not stifle private sector initiative.

2) *Management and Ownership of Local Facilitator companies*

Each local facilitator company will issue the majority of its issued shares to the International Facilitator Ltd. Each local facilitator company will designate:

- One seat on the board for an International Facilitator Ltd. representative if their constitution allows voting according to share ownership, OR
- A majority of seats on the board will be designated to International Facilitator Ltd. if the constitution does not allow voting according to share ownership.

Each local facilitator company will adhere to the majority decisions of the International Facilitator Ltd. board.

3) *Finance*

The financial year of each company or organisation will be established and annual audits prepared and a copy submitted to International Facilitator Ltd.

Any dividends deriving from profits or cash surpluses of local facilitator companies will be allocated as follows:

- At least 50 per cent of the cash surplus will be reinvested in new or existing service ventures.
- At least 10 per cent of the cash surplus will be allocated to staff bonuses.
- The remaining cash reserve will be utilized as agreed by the shareholders of each company.

4) *Confidentiality of internal Local Facilitator documents*

Business documents provided by International Facilitator Ltd. or sister local facilitator companies that are designated as internal documents will be utilized by each company for internal purposes only. These documents will not be passed to any individual, company or organization outside the local facilitator network without authorization from the author of the material.

5) *Reporting*

Each local facilitator company will prepare a six-monthly report detailing the past and future activities, plans and finances of the company. This report will be submitted to each board member of the International Facilitator Ltd. by 30 April and 31 October of each year.

5. Early Experience in Market Development: Introducing New Services

THIS NEW BDS APPROACH involves moving away from direct, donor-funded supply of services, towards the establishment of a more dynamic relationship with commercial providers already present in the marketplace.

The FIT programme in Uganda and Zimbabwe is undertaking interesting experiments in the commercial provision of BDS services – there are signs that other FIT affiliates may soon join them. Thus far, three experiments to introduce new services commercially are underway:

- In Zimbabwe, a business-to-business advertising paper is produced in-house to introduce a new service to the marketplace. In this case the service is new and the provider has yet to be created or identified.
- In Uganda, business tours were offered commercially through a joint venture with a travel agency – the new focus is on facilitating such tours for many agencies. Here there were potential providers (travel agencies), but no one who had ever offered the service before.
- Also in Uganda, a commercial radio station is launching a small business radio show. The provider exists and offers similar services, but has not offered this particular service product to SEs.

In Kenya, ApproTEC offers new service products and more to existing providers. A package of technology, product marketing, and training is offered to manufacturers, retailers, and SE customers. Both supply and demand are addressed, but the centre of all the interventions is a new product.

In the ApproTEC case, business development services are delivered through a commercial relationship that closely resembles a franchise. In southern Africa, SEs that establish linkage contracts with other firms can also access credit or business development services from the buyer to whom they supply goods or services. Once the business community is aware of the potential benefits of linkages, the need for the project-sponsored service disappears. Market-specific BDS continues to be delivered within linkage contracts.

Efforts to develop markets for BDS in collaboration with commercial providers are all fairly new and no hard conclusions can yet be drawn, but some indications are clear. All of these examples address the development of markets for BDS more than building the capacity or sustainability of specific providers. However, where a service is new it may be more expedient to function as a provider for a limited time and in a limited manner in order to demonstrate the potential. The first case study comes from Harare, Zimbabwe in late 1998 and early 1999, where a new service was being offered to the market in a climate of rising inflation and uncertainty. The cases are categorized according to the status of the service and the providers, as suggested in Table 4.2.

New Service, New Providers

FIT's demonstration of Business Connect, Zimbabwe

Building on research undertaken by FIT in a number of countries, FIT Zimbabwe, with support from the Austrian government, decided to produce 'a customer-focused business-to-business advertising paper connecting micro- and small enterprises to medium and large companies.' Market studies by FIT suggested that there was demand among SEs for market information and market linkages, and that large businesses were interested in advertising targeted at the SE market, while small businesses recognized the need for low-cost advertising.[16]

Previous commercial providers of a similar product in Harare were unsuccessful. Efforts to find a joint venture partner failed, so FIT Zimbabwe decided to produce the paper in-house. The product could thus be developed quickly and flexibly, responding to turbulent markets and the high expectations among larger businesses for timely advertising. After the product is developed, i.e. profitable, FIT Zimbabwe is considering a number of potential exit strategies to relinquish its role as provider (see below for more detail).

In the meantime, most production is outsourced to avoid the purchase of costly equipment. The minimal staff required are clearly tied to *Business Connect* by virtue of their skills and contracts, and bookkeeping is separate. This helps FIT Zimbabwe keep track of the real costs of developing and producing the paper, and maintains a structure that can spin off into the private sector. To this degree the role of facilitator and the role of provider are kept distinct.

Results so far

The paper was registered in December 1998 and is currently printing monthly with a print-run of about 10 000 copies distributed to businesses in and around Harare. By the sixth issue, 97 per cent of operating costs were being covered by income generated from advertising. The early success of the paper should be measured against the general economic conditions in the country, which include high inflation and declining foreign investment. Benefits have been noted for small businesses already, including:

- A security company reports an increase in business due to advertising and has requested a long-term advertising contract.

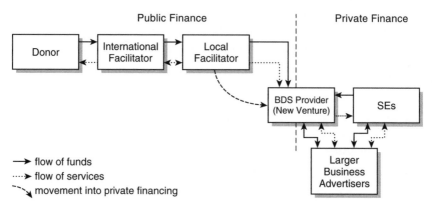

Figure 5.1: *Business Connect: The start of a new venture?*

- A small insurance company (Aggressive Insurance Brokers) has linked with an SE association to market insurance packages designed specifically for them.
- The Confederation of Zimbabwe Industries, which facilitates the Small Business Linkage Programme,[17] distributes copies to its members and publicizes business linkage and training opportunities through advertisements.
- A paint company is purchasing chemicals from a small supplier in a rural town.

With *Business Connect*, a win/win opportunity has been identified and appears profitable. Advertising sales agents are able to sell advertisements to large businesses by demonstrating how well they reach SEs. Without any specific planning on the part of the facilitator, the paper helps to address job quality issues by bringing insurance agents in contact with SE associations, as well as serving the advertising needs of a linkage programme run by a regional chamber of industry that targets SEs. Because they purchase smaller black and white or group advertisements, SEs pay less than the large companies. For most SEs, it is their first experience of using print media to advertise, and they are surprised by the positive impact.

Business Connect presently straddles a temporary line between public and private sector financing. It has begun to take the shape of a new business, in as far as three staff have been hired and they relate to their clients as staff of *Business Connect*. While still an activity of the facilitator (product development), the paper is well grounded in the private sector. Most of its production is outsourced, the sales agents operate in line with the local market, and the paper is covering all production and most staff costs. Figure 5.1 presents a diagram of the venture.

The future relationship between FIT Zimbabwe and Business Connect

FIT Zimbabwe would like to see the idea of the paper copied by others, to develop the market for advertising; but this idea is countered by a reluctance to subject the paper to competition and thus reduce its potential profitability. Deciding when the product is complete enough to prove viable in the private sector is a major concern. At the time of writing, FIT Zimbabwe has decided to support the paper until it is able to cover all of its operating costs and generate profits, which it expects to take about another four months, if the business climate does not deteriorate further.

The 'founder syndrome' – the reluctance to let what is essentially a new business go – raises the question of whether the facilitator needs to exit completely from the provider role. Would it be possible for the company to retain some interest in provider companies it helped to start?

If FIT Zimbabwe does not make *Business Connect* independent, donor financing may create a monopoly, or give an unfair advantage that stifles other initiatives. It may also result in high costs that render the whole paper unmarketable. Its style or content may change subtly in response to donors instead of to the local business community. There is also the fact that staff have been willing to work hard for less, in the hope that they could have a stake in owning the paper. How can their hard work be rewarded and what security do they have when the paper is no longer a product of FIT Zimbabwe? To answer all of these concerns, a number of options are under consideration.

- Setting up a joint venture with a private sector partner was rejected. This would have meant that FIT Zimbabwe retained interest in the paper, as half-owner of a provider.
- Licensing the product and selling rights to use the format, templates, and idea of the paper depends on profitability for a certain period, and the name and reputation of the paper. It has a defined exit strategy. As long as conditions of the licence were respected, FIT Zimbabwe would not provide services. It could offer the licence freely to any provider, or at a subsidized rate to target a particular group of SEs, and so adjust its impact on the market.
- Establishing a new venture owned by FIT Zimbabwe by majority shares but managed separately. FIT Zimbabwe would only sit on the board of directors and receive any share dividends. Founding *Business Connect* staff would receive limited share allocations. Profits would be reinvested in the paper or would support FIT Zimbabwe's activities.

Staff currently prefer the third option. If the paper earns profits, it could enable FIT Zimbabwe to pursue opportunities to develop the BDS market more flexibly than when working for donors. However, even as directors,

FIT Zimbabwe might be tempted to maintain a monopoly on the market. The development agenda and profit agenda could potentially conflict.

Other options considered include:

- A franchise relationship whereby FIT Zimbabwe offers training, templates, regional advertisements, and ongoing support to franchisees around the country or in neighbouring countries. Unlike licensing, FIT Zimbabwe would continue to invest in and support the franchisees. They would still have to monitor their impact on the market, since they would still be operating both as a facilitator and a provider of a national or regional information and advertising service. Eventually, the entire franchise could be sold.
- Selling the company to the highest bidder; or to the highest quality partner (possibly for a lower price); or to a provider prepared to sign a contract to continue directing advertisement to and for SEs. At present, this is the commercial advantage *Business Connect* has over other advertising media. The contract could also ensure that management information is shared with FIT Zimbabwe in order to provide impact data for FIT. By selling, FIT Zimbabwe or the *Business Connect* staff could also retain partial ownership through shares.

Whichever option is adopted, the ideal solution will keep the service in the market place commercially without compromising FIT Zimbabwe's responsibilities as a facilitator.

New service, new and existing providers

FIT's joint venture and introduction of business tours in Uganda

Tradeway Tours was a joint venture launched with a travel agency by FIT Uganda, to promote business tours to Kenya and South Africa. The experience was one of the programme's first efforts to introduce a new commercial service and it folded in less than six months – possibly because it lacked the right blend of capital, skills and contacts to succeed.

In summary, as a 50 per cent partner of a commercial provider, FIT Uganda was not successful. In its role as a *facilitator*, FIT Uganda did very well. The introduction of a new product was very successful. Eight commercial agents sought information from FIT to organize tours themselves, and four agencies began openly competing.[19] The Chamber of Commerce, which offers subsidized tours, was also interested. Competitors generally offered the new product to the more privileged SEs, but once tours were no longer offered or advertised with FIT's support, they tended to stop offering them as well.

Thus, FIT Uganda's role as facilitator continues, supplying the local travel industry with information on tours and potential clients. The unit still sees mass market potential for tours that match the needs of smaller SEs, and wants to demonstrate that potential to commercial agents.

Joint ventures are not necessarily the best partnership structure

FIT Uganda believes that joint ventures can work where capital and risk are the major constraints on providing the service. Here, the constraints were simply lack of information and product development. However, the following lessons were learned:

- It takes time to select a partner and establish a new company, while markets are highly dynamic – before the partner is found the business opportunity may be lost.
- Donor funding needs to be very flexible to allow both partners to create a profitable base.
- The new company suffers all the risks of any new small business, and both partners have to agree on how to take risks and find ways to respond constructively to market opportunities.
- A common management culture between two companies may be difficult to achieve.

If the venture is commercially successful, there is a danger that the facilitator role may be engulfed by the desire to become a profitable provider.

As is evident in Figure 5.2, the joint venture was balanced on the line between public and private finance, and between development and profit agendas. It faced competition from other commercial agencies and the Chamber of Commerce, and was under pressure to focus on smaller SEs.

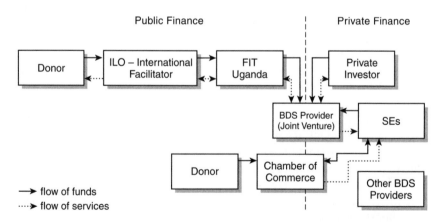

Figure 5.2: *Tradeways Tours – joint venture in a competitive market*

Further product development and facilitation of tours

Exchange visits facilitated by NGOs have now evolved into business tours, but much remains to be done in developing products for particular micro- or small enterprise market niches. Package tours for micro-enterprises have been developed in Kenya. They have been tested and the initial impact evaluated with business people from Kenya, Tanzania, and Uganda. They are currently being developed in Zimbabwe. Whether the tours can be marketed profitably to SEs is still unclear, but indications from Tanzania and Zimbabwe, where commercial transport and travel operators are developing (or offering) tours with little or no intervention from FIT after an initial trial period, suggest that they can.

Experience has shown that travel agencies are prepared to adjust their operations to accommodate a new type of package tour, slightly expanding their client base, but are not eager to change their market niche or specialization significantly. Nor were they willing to develop or identify tours, even if they had the facilities. FIT Uganda hopes to play this role, therefore, and subsequently to identify a commercial means of keeping the service in the market.

Upgraded service, existing providers

Launching a small-business radio show in Uganda

Radio is popular even in the poorest households, and accessible to those who cannot read. FIT Uganda thus considered that a small business radio show was potentially viable. They obtained funds to conduct market research,[20] which backed up their theory, and also helped determine the style, content, sources of information and potential sponsor for the initial shows. It is hoped the concept will have a long-lasting effect among the existing providers.

FIT helped to design the format for the show, and is also helping with production of a test demo and the first two shows. They are offering only their time, SE contacts, and ideas to the station – no financing. A donor pays for FIT's input, so the provider is receiving a business idea, and limited consultancy services.

The show will include regular free slots for businesses wishing to advertise opportunities for SEs (wholesalers, suppliers of materials, customers, etc.). It will also give SEs a chance publicly to air their views on current issues which affects their businesses, a need SEs stressed during market research.

The intervention is low cost and unlikely to do harm. The broadcasting of potentially valuable commercial information to and from SEs may help them boost their profits or form new commercial relationships with suppliers and customers. SEs also gain a voice in civil society, a positive aspect of a development agenda that seeks to empower those not usually heard.

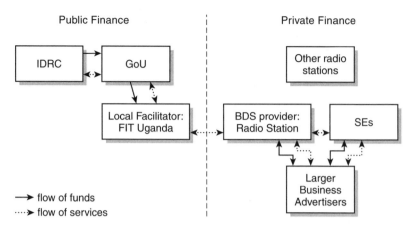

Figure 5.3: *Business information for SEs via a radio show*

Market research covered the radio market, SE listeners, and potential advertisers, to develop a shortlist of potential providers. A popular, credible, radio station with a history of not being afraid to raise controversy, was chosen. FIT Uganda persuaded the management of the selected station that the show would be an important business opportunity. They stressed the market potential of the listener segment (SEs), and the interest large companies might have in reaching this market.

Only one commercial provider was approached. This may give the impression that the provider was offered an unfair market advantage, but FIT Uganda's assistance was confined to limited market research and the start of product development, so the offer involved only the cost of their consultancy services for the number of days involved. The show's commercial value hinges on the advertising revenue the station can generate, which depends on its own contacts, reputation, technical capacity and commitment to the product. FIT Uganda also stated it will probably be interested in selling assistance to other radio stations to develop similar shows, after proof of viability (or after a stated time period). In the radio industry, as soon as the 'product' is in the marketplace, the idea becomes public property and can be copied and adapted. As the FIT manager explains:

> We hope that by successfully establishing one radio programme we will stimulate demand for our support from other companies. We will test the demand for advertising to small business to assess one important component for media development targeted at small business. Our market assessment is being undertaken by test-marketing the programme with one provider. We hope to evaluate the niche and identify other interested providers.

The radio show and the advertising paper illustrate the potential for using the interests of large businesses to deliver BDS to smaller businesses. Large businesses have difficulty reaching smaller businesses, particularly SEs, which are geographically dispersed, not necessarily literate, and may not respond to mainstream advertising. FIT Uganda has knowledge and contacts within the SE 'sector'. If they can capture the attention of SEs, larger enterprises are willing to pay for advertising or market research services. The money generated from the sales to larger enterprises can be used to cross-subsidize less expensive or, in the case of the radio show, even free advertising for SEs. In both Uganda and Zimbabwe, the main challenge is the ability to reach and encourage SEs to experience the benefits of advertising, not to get advertising income from larger enterprises.

New service, existing providers

Support services in the context of a commercial relationship: ApproTEC's technology and market development

In Kenya, an NGO called ApproTEC places technology development within the marketplace by developing locally manufactured tools and technology to create profitable businesses for retailers, manufacturers, and purchasers of the products. Founded in 1991, ApproTEC designs and develops tools using locally available inputs, which can create or support businesses for farmers or entrepreneurs: an oil press with a gravity filter, a tool to make earth/concrete building blocks and a water pump that uses a foot pedal to pump water for irrigation or other uses.

Market research shows the technology needed to boost business for SEs or farmers. It takes about a year to design the product professionally, and this requires significant investment and expertise. Selected local manufacturers then receive a package of tools, manuals, training, quality control and

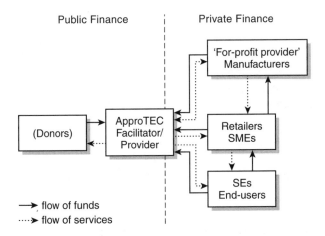

Figure 5.4: *Developing disseminating technology in a market context*

marketing services. They sell their ApproTEC-approved products to selected retailers, who also receive training and marketing services carried out on their behalf by ApproTEC (radio and newspaper, mobile demonstrations, trade fairs).

The package of services and the relationship established with small private sector manufacturers closely resembles a franchise: ApproTEC receives a percentage of the selling price of the final product – about 15 per cent of the final price of the oil press, and about 25 per cent of the water pump, for example. ApproTEC also trains SEs to use and maintain the tools. The business services provided cater to the local market conditions for specific products or services.

Originally, ApproTEC encouraged manufacturers to deal with retailers directly, but lessons learned led the organization to place itself between retailers and manufacturers as a master dealer and distributor. In this way, it can supply retailers on credit and also assure its commission. Freelance sales people also sell ApproTEC products for commission. A newsletter provides customers, retailers and manufacturers with information about the product and contains examples of SEs, farmers or retailers who have developed successful businesses. SE customers are eligible for training from ApproTEC, for which they pay a nominal fee. ApproTEC also provides services for donors, such as extensive impact monitoring.[21]

Perhaps most important for all actors and many possible copycats, ApproTEC looks for products that can capitalize on local business opportunities. Pedal pumps were designed around the time that liberalized air cargo costs went down and outlets for small farmers selling export-quality vegetables rose dramatically. When edible oil prices were liberalized and raw imports taxed, ApproTEC saw the potential market for locally produced seed oil. They invested significant (donor) resources in the design of the oil press, and produced a press, which is at least 40 per cent more effective than other manual presses.

ApproTEC receives about US$65 for each pump sold and US$470 for each press, in 1998 prices. After two years of sales, over 800 presses had been sold in Kenya alone, and after three years of sales, over 5000 water pumps in East and Central Africa region. The income earned does not cover all the costs ApproTEC incurs to support the project, but with larger production and distribution, training and customer support services devolved to retailers, potentially it could.[22]

From a market development perspective, it might be worthwhile to try outsourcing some of the services that ApproTEC provides, such as marketing, distribution, information provision, or training. Like any firm considering a linkage contract, the benefits of allowing other providers in must be weighed against the possible loss of the close fit between production, distribution, and market demand that a franchiser-like provider can offer. From the market development perspective, it is also important to make sure that local inventors, retailers and manufacturers of products like ApproTEC's are not subjected to unfair competition. If the franchise-like part of Appro-TEC were commercially viable it could separate itself into an independent for-profit company, enabling ApproTEC the NGO facilitator to continue to use donor resources to develop new products without concern about negative market distortion.

New and existing services, new and existing providers

Facilitating business linkages in Southern Africa

Business linkages have been defined as 'ongoing commercial dealings between separate profit-oriented enterprises' ... the positive result of market forces compelling businesses to seek the most efficient means of sourcing the components and services they require to produce the products and services they sell. Good business linkages result in specialization, diversification, improved efficiency, and benefits for all parties (Grierson et al., 1999). Business linkages are at the heart of developing a vibrant, diverse market for BDS.

Linkage contracts can be an effective means of delivering BDS that is firmly rooted in a real market context. Larger businesses (buyers) may save on costs and increase their profits in ways that benefit small businesses (suppliers), particularly when the buyer offers mentoring, training, credit or materials. A contract with a well-known large enterprise also can also help a small enterprise's credit rating. A win/win situation is formalized.

South Africa study suggests profit motive yields higher social and economic returns

Linkages are sometimes targeted by development agents to benefit marginalized or historically disadvantaged business people. Research suggests, however, that linkages motivated primarily by charitable concerns are likely to fail. As with all the interventions advocated here, the starting point should be the market. A 1998 study of 75 large firms in South Africa found that the most productive and efficient linkages are motivated by a mutual desire for higher profits. If a buyer does not believe it will profit from a linkage, and is trying it only out of charity or for political considerations, or if the supplier feels they have a historical right to the relationship, neither side is likely to take the steps needed to ensure that the outcome is positive.

Equal relationships with opportunities for capacity building are the most profitable for all parties

In the case of franchising, the franchiser is dependent on the success of its franchisees, and the relationship is ongoing. When subcontracting or unbundling, the buyer of the service tends to be a large business, and usually has much more power than the supplier to dictate the terms of the contract. Research in South Africa and elsewhere suggests, however, that both the most efficient and most profitable linkages occur when the buyer and the supplier have a more equal partnership, and each tries to assist the other to ensure that the contract is mutually satisfactory. Contracts that enabled suppliers to build capacity also yielded the highest benefits for both sides. This was confirmed by the project experience outlined below.

The Manicaland Linkage Project – linkages survive economic downturn

In Manica province of Zimbabwe, the Manicaland Chamber of Industries, a regional branch of the Confederation of Zimbabwe Industries, has helped to facilitate 139 linkages in the pilot phase of a business linkage project funded by NORAD.[23] The project began in November 1997 when the timber industry was expanding. The timber sector accounted for 94 of the 139 linkages, with 76 of these under two large firms. For one of the firms, an effort to unbundle their engineering workshop reduced costs by about 20 per cent. In 1998, the economy took a downturn, with rising inflation and interests rates, and contracting markets. In spite of all the problems, as of August 1998, all but one of the linkage contracts was still underway. Business linkages remained an efficient way of dealing with a difficult economic situation.

Facilitator offers a discrete set of services to change the business culture

In the Manicaland project, the regional chamber of industries plays the role of facilitator. It is careful to facilitate linkages without positioning itself between the buyer and suppliers. An office (with only one senior staff member and one support staff member), aims to facilitate linkages with a minimum of interventions, including buyer/supplier workshops (essentially the same as the brokering workshops set up under FIT in Kenya and Ghana, organized around a particular sub-sector); buyer 'open houses', where small groups of potential suppliers visit interested buyers; feasibility studies, to assess the potential for a particular linkage; and supplier capacity audits, where needs for supplier capacity-building are identified. Capacity-building is generally undertaken by the buyer involved. In addition, the linkages concept was promoted through print media campaigns. After the pilot phase, it appeared that many of the potential suppliers were well aware of the potential benefits of linkages.

Supplier-provided BDS a key factor in commercial success

In Zimbabwe, mentoring was institutionalized. The two largest suppliers each assigned at least one staff member to oversee the contracts and identify new ones, as well as identifying ways of helping their suppliers succeed. The

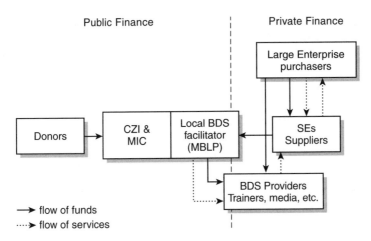

Figure 5.5: *Manicaland Business Linkages Project*

project shows how a facilitator could come in for a short time to demonstrate the advantages to business of establishing linkages, and then provide assistance in helping them do it. Once the business community has recognized the advantages, the facilitator is no longer necessary. In the case of Manicaland, the Chamber of Industries could soon safely move into a regulatory and advocacy role.

Evidence of a correlation between SE productivity and job quality

A possible criticism is that the buyer's economic motivation may be to avoid taxes or compliance with labour legislation. The South Africa study found evidence of this in 'many' of the linkage contracts. They also found that a 'significant number' of SE suppliers paid all relevant taxes and fees while employing workers who were members of unions and covered by the standard labour benefits. Furthermore, these were generally the most efficient of the small suppliers, and the ones that were growing the most rapidly – evidence of a correlation between SE productivity or growth and job quality.

New or existing services, new Providers

The potential for franchising

Franchising is rapidly becoming one of the private sector's most effective means of disseminating business expertise and support to small-scale business people in industrialized countries. In a franchise relationship, unlike sub-contracting or licensing arrangements, the success of the franchiser and the franchisees are structurally interlinked, and a win/win approach is institutionalized.[24] The franchiser's profits depend on how well the franchisees manage their independent businesses. Typically, the franchiser provides assistance in marketing, training, access to supplies, occasionally start-up capital, and ongoing management support. Franchisees supply local knowledge, often a small amount of capital, and motivation. The percentage or amount of regular payment from franchisee to franchiser varies considerably. Increasingly, international franchisers are creating linkages in developing countries through franchises, and many developing countries are setting up their own franchises.

Telecommunications is an area where the franchising model has proven very productive in developing countries. Phone shops, selling basic telecommunications services, for example, have been established through a number of franchises (Barton and Bear, 1999). In India, 10 000 franchisees are part of the Teleport network. Vodacom in South Africa has 375 phone shops established in three years by 250 franchisees. In Senegal, the franchise was established by the national telecommunications operator, Sonatel, with over 1000 shops; a similar arrangement exists in Indonesia. In these cases, the telecommunications provider offers training, management support, and some financial assistance to franchisees. Much of the risk and the labour involved in starting up a business are reduced with a franchise. Large amounts of capital can be invested where it is most needed, taking full advantage of economies of scale, and the investment from the network of franchisees can be directed. In the case of the telecommunications franchises, the telecommunications company can direct its capital to central infrastructure, technology, advertising and delivery of basic services, while the franchisees invest in sales offices and customer service.

Business Connect may or may not prove to be a good model for franchising – its profitability is not yet established and it may not be easy to replicate while maintaining the unique selling points and quality. However, efforts to find ways to replicate profitable business support services through a franchise should be explored. As a number of advocates have noted, the model is potentially effective and profitable for all parties (Barton, 1997). In terms of the BDS it offers retailers and manufacturers, ApproTEC has set up the structure and services of a franchise. All that remains would be for it to spin off or expand its franchiser role so that its own commercial future depended on the success of its franchisees.

Synopsis: developing products and advocating for change: commercial and non-commercial facilitators

The first four cases presented here demonstrated new service products to a local market. Tour agencies offered tourist packages, but not business tours. Newspapers were offering advertising, but not advertising targeted at small businesses and not with a focus on business opportunities. Oil presses were available: the franchise-like package of training, technology, and marketing services available to manufacturers and retailers was new. The services could be called service 'products', because they were developed, tested and refined to meet the needs of a particular market.

This is an appropriate role for a commercial facilitator, so long as the facilitator makes restrained use of donor funds, without attempting to gain an ongoing market share. The development of a new service product is a sometimes risky and expensive proposition; demonstrating the value of an unproven product is possibly less expensive (depending on the product) but also useful because it lowers the risk for private sector actors. Impact on the market has to be continually monitored until the product is taken up by the private sector. Should it prove necessary for the organization that developed the new product also to be involved in its ongoing delivery, the facilitator could sell the service product, spin off a private commercial company or franchise, or abandon its role as facilitator and become a commercial provider.

In Manica Region, the facilitation of linkages by the Chamber of Industries was not a new service product per se, but an attempt to change business culture by demonstrating BDS that could be delivered within a contractual relationship between the buyer and supplier. Services, such as advertising, training and capacity audit were supplied by the project and proved useful in changing the business culture. While a commercial enterprise could facilitate linkages, the role is an appropriate one for a public body such as the Chamber of Industries.

In many cases, however, the private sector is already offering some version of the 'product', and delivery systems are numerous, ranging from highly formal and expensive establishments catering to the upper end of the market, to the most informal where relationships and favours are a more common currency than cash. This is the case of training, where private sector trainers and establishments abound, both in the formal sector, where they face a different policy and regulatory environment, and in the informal sector, where they operate solely according to market forces.[25] The next chapter explores ways to improve existing services that are already being provided by the private sector.

6.   Early Experience in Market Development: Improving Existing Services

Improving Supply: Indigenous Capacity Building

GOVERNMENT-SPONSORED PROVISION OF TRAINING in technical, managerial and commercial skills for small enterprises has often proved poor value for money. It has also tended to be supply oriented, and thus out of tune with real market opportunities. The result is that for training with a broad outreach, high quality and market relevance, many look to the private sector, and governments are now seeking to cultivate such training. In a climate of decreasing donor finance, NGOs or other publicly funded institutions may become more like the private sector with time, but for now, there is a large difference in the cost.

Private sector trainers are paid according to the local economy, at prices their clients can afford. Independent trainers in Uganda were found to be earning US$80-160 per month from their training activities (low fees in rural areas meant the number of trainees were higher), slightly more than a teacher might earn. Training institutes paid US$40-80 per month to their predominantly part-time trainers. The range of incomes found in Zimbabwe was larger, and not well reported, but trainers at the bottom end were earning as little as US$50 a month. In contrast, trainers paid by development agencies earn in the range of US$100-250 per day.

This less formal end of the spectrum of private sector trainers has remained largely invisible to development agents until recently. This may well be the part of the sector that has the best potential for reaching a significant number of SEs sustainably. In contrast, traditional apprentice training has been widely studied and is well documented. In sub-Saharan Africa, the apprenticeship system probably provides more vocational training than all of the formal institutions combined, particularly in West Africa.

Yet, few projects have sought practical ways to enhance the existing system. In Kenya, Ghana, and Zimbabwe some donors have researched, planned and even implemented activities to improve the quality or outreach of apprentice training, but the results of the experience are not easily available.

New service, new and existing providers

FIT's work with for-profit trainers in Uganda, Zimbabwe and Kenya
Identifying the sector

After realizing that small-scale, for-profit business skills trainers who market their services directly to SEs are prevalent in Uganda, the FIT programme

Box 6.1: 'Back-street' trainers – some cross-country comparisons

In towns, 'back-street' training companies and consultants offer a wide range of courses, covering both business skills (accountancy, marketing, import-export trading, clearing and forwarding, business planning and administration, etc.) and vocational skills (hairdressing, tailoring, hotel and tourism, food production, wood and metal work, etc.) In the rural areas, individual resource people (sometimes termed 'grassroots' or 'barefoot' trainers) offer training, particularly general business skills training, to SEs, while traditional apprenticeships provide the bulk of technical training.

More courses were found in Uganda than in a more rigorous study in Zimbabwe. This might be partly because public-sector provision is less developed in Uganda, and partly because the regulatory environment in Zimbabwe does not make life easy for the smallest trainers. Also, in Uganda small-scale private trainers offer management training. In Zimbabwe management training is available in the larger-scale, formal private training sector. Zimbabwe, on the other hand, has more computer training than Uganda, perhaps because of cheaper costs of importing the machines from South Africa. Around Nairobi's neighbourhoods a wide range of training is on offer – computer training appears popular even in the poorest areas. Computer training and food catering were the most common training establishments in all neighbourhoods surveyed.

undertook surveys in Uganda, Zimbabwe and Kenya to learn more about this 'invisible' informal side of private sector training.[26] The surveys excluded trainers usually hired by publicly funded institutions (including churches, NGOs and projects), and did not include the 'master crafts-people' of apprentice systems. In Uganda, 160 independent trainers and 89 small-scale private training institutions were identified. In Zimbabwe, 90 small training businesses were identified; cross-checking with a DFID-supported study of private sector training institutes (Bennell, 1997) revealed an additional 32. In Kenya, the study confined itself to rapid rural appraisal of what could visibly be seen to be on offer in a number of low-income or semi-rural neighbourhoods around Nairobi. Thirty-seven establishments were identified in Kikuyu, Riuru township, Banana township, and East Lee. Sixty establishments were identified in the middle-class neighbourhoods of Buru Buru and Langata West.

In Uganda, the survey revealed that rural areas generally had as many, if not more trainers per capita, than urban areas. In Zimbabwe, the survey, though brief, covered the entire country, including every major town. Again, there were more trainers per capita in many of the rural areas than in the large urban centres. In Kenya, the survey covered only a cross-section of neighbourhoods around Nairobi, and did not attempt a comprehensive

Table 6.1: Courses provided by small-scale for-profit trainers

	Uganda	Zimbabwe	Four Nairobi rural and low income neighbourhoods
Number of courses surveyed	352	167	50
Management-related skills (%)			
Business mgmt. and admin.	17	5	Na
Marketing	8	6	Na
Bookkeeping, accounting	17	1	Na
Misc. specific management (e.g. clearing & forwarding)	3	0	Na
Total % management-related skills	45	12	12
Vocational skills (%)			
Secretarial	12	17	14
Computer-related	10	35	12
Dressmaking, tailoring	5	27	16
Woodwork	9	1	6
Metalwork	6	1	0
Mechanics	4	3	12
Building, electrics, catering, hair dressing, photography, driving	9	4	28
Total % vocational skills	55	88	88
Totals	100	100	100

overview of the country.

Training and training establishments in all three countries offered a wide range of courses. In Kenya computer training, hairdressing and catering were abundant. Training in computer skills was available even in the most unlikely neighbourhoods where electricity is uncommon. Table 6.1 outlines the kinds of training on offer in Zimbabwe and Uganda, and gives a suggestion of what can be found in low-income neighbourhoods near or within Nairobi.

In Uganda and Zimbabwe, an active effort was needed to find these trainers; they often advertise only by word of mouth, as they cater for training needs in their immediate locality. In Kenya, the sector operates openly; structures to regulate the industry exist, but do not sanction those who do not comply. In Zimbabwe, there is active sanctioning of unlicensed training without formal premises. A survey by Bennell et al. (1999) in Tanzania found for-profit unregistered training institutes outnumbered registered ones in

Arusha and Kilimanjaro, but in Dar es Salaam most were registered. These businesses thrive without any external funding from donors.

The quality question – more consumer information and less government regulation

The quality of the training provided varies greatly, but strong government regulation (as in Zimbabwe) probably only drives trainers 'underground'. Providing consumer information may be the easiest way to enable the market to regulate itself better.

Advantages of small-scale for-profit training

Training proposed by private trainers to SEs is affordable, conveniently located and has many of the advantages outlined in Chapter 4 for service provision by commercial providers in general, including the following:

- When offered in local languages it is easier to learn and ask questions; owners of SEs in all three countries were very enthusiastic about training in their own languages.
- The training can respond to the immediate needs and opportunities of SEs in a given location.
- If the trainee customers are not satisfied, they can put peer pressure on the trainer to improve.
- The training can become a vehicle for business relationships and networks that are mutually beneficial to SE trainers and SE trainees.

Training by women and for women

Female trainers have been prominent in surveys and FIT pilots. When empowering women is part of the development agenda, support to the smaller and more informal end of private sector training is likely to reach female trainers. Most studies indicate that women are at least well represented in the sector, both as trainers and as owners of training institutes. In some places, female trainers may outnumber males. In Africa, the majority of small-scale entrepreneurs are also women, so in traditional societies where men and women do not interact freely, female trainers may be more effective at training women.

The importance of a shared social world – networks and customer orientation

The fact that the trainer is part of the same social and business environment as the SEs is very significant. Opportunities for networking and tailor-made services abound. The example in Box 6.2, where a trainer offers three different BDS services to her clients (training, free business counselling, and sale of management aids), is not uncommon.

Building the capacity of micro-scale business skills trainers

The FIT programme aims to improve the training offered by small-scale local trainers. The best strategy to improve the quality of training may be to address the weaknesses that trainers want to improve, and are willing to invest in. In Uganda and Zimbabwe, trainers expressed demand for new courses to offer to micro- and small enterprise clients (see Mbeine and Andersen, 1998). FIT Uganda offered training-of-trainers (ToT) courses in: Rapid Market Appraisal (RMA), User-Led Innovation (ULI) and Grass-roots Management Training (GMT).[27] FIT Zimbabwe offered training in RMA in 1999. All three ToT courses are short, and help entrepreneurs to become more market oriented in their businesses.

Despite their very modest incomes (US$150 a month in rural areas of Kenya and Uganda), trainers have been willing to pay around US$40 for RMA and ULI course in Uganda, and around US$70 for GMT. In Zimbabwe, they paid 1000 Zimbabwe dollars (US$27). In Uganda, the first six months of training of SEs in RMA or ULI was supported by a subsidy scheme that also helped FIT Uganda monitor the results of the ToT. During the pilot period of $6\frac{1}{2}$ months, over 500 SEs were involved in training or workshops organized by the eight active trainers. A wide geographic area was covered with training activities taking place in seven districts of Uganda. Over 70 per cent of the training was undertaken outside Kampala and 50 per cent outside the major towns, organized in church halls or small community centres and offered at a competitive price.

Trainers found the initial marketing of courses and activities difficult, but there was a steady growth in the number of courses as difficulties were overcome (see Figure 6.1). By the end of the monitoring period, 55 SEs a week were being trained. The subsidy that FIT Uganda offered trainers to help them develop markets for the their new product proved to be expensive to implement; some trainers did not bother to collect it.[28]

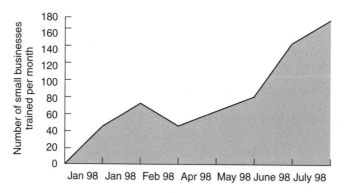

Figure 6.1: *Graph detailing the growth in business training activities of eight training businesses over a six-month period*

Box 6.2: The Story of a For-profit Trainer

In Uganda Mary operates a peanut-butter production enterprise – she supplies three local supermarkets – and runs a training business, which is her main source of income. Her experience as a trainer began when she was accepted for a Training of Trainers (ToT) course to offer Improve Your Business (IYB) to her fellow SEs. Since then, she has attended two ToT courses sold by FIT Uganda: Rapid Market Appraisal (RMA) and Grassroots Management Training (GMT). She reports that the latter are more suited to her clients because they do not require literacy. She is able, at times, to get financial assistance in offering IYB courses, but 'If I cannot get sponsorship, I just charge the full costs.' In fact, Mary earned more on her IYB courses before she had access to the subsidy, because her trainees were willing to pay more when there was no donor involved.

For GMT and RMA no subsidy is available, but: 'this is not a problem because the SEs are willing to pay anyway, especially those who cannot read and write, because they realize much better that they need the course.' In fact, Mary says that the poorest clients are often the most eager to pay because they have been excluded from funded training programmes, which normally require some degree of literacy.

Training in management skills is more lucrative than the highly competitive peanut butter business, but Mary says, 'I keep the peanut butter production because it helps me be accepted among my training customers.' Her customers appreciate the fact that her training is offered from a small-business base. Recently she asked a group of business people from the neighbouring region why they had initially been reluctant to try her training, but had later become extremely enthusiastic. They said they were wary of trainers who came from far to 'use us to make lots of money' (from donors). Once they realized that Mary was just like them, a small business person with her own simple training business, they were eager to learn from her.

One of Mary's objectives is to develop and maintain long-term business relationships. She visits her clients regularly to provide free business advice, for several reasons. First, she wants to ensure that the students absorb the lessons she teaches so that they can see results from the training. This improves her image as a trainer and makes her feel that her efforts are worthwhile. Second, the visits help her improve her business network, so she can sell more courses and manage-ment materials. 'I sell stock cards and cash books which I print myself. Small business people often don't want to sit down and make them themselves.' Thus Mary offers three services to SEs – micro-consultancy, supply of management aids, and training – while developing business networks that benefit herself and her clients.

FIT in Uganda and Zimbabwe is at present investigating ways to develop networks of commercial trainers to facilitate the provision of services to strengthen their capacities. Trainers expressed interest in the following services:

- ToT courses in new skills and training methodologies
- refresher and upgrading courses
- group advertising of training services
- certification of training courses which meet agreed standards
- publication of a directory of private-sector training facilities
- facilitation of resource-sharing among institutes (e.g. secondment of part-time trainers).

Enforcement of regulations is a problem is most countries; but it may also be the case that apparently low-quality training may match market requirements and purchasing power. Nevertheless, in both formal and informal sectors, trainers of all levels showed interest in ToT courses and reported a lack of training materials (books, guides), on the market.

Existing service, existing providers

Stimulating the demand: a voucher programme in Paraguay

Thus far, all of the examples presented have primarily addressed the problems concerning the supply of BDS. Meanwhile, demand for BDS is being developed by voucher programmes in Peru, El Salvador, Argentina, Ecuador, and Kenya. Most are modelled on a programme set up by the Inter-American Development Bank (IDB) in Paraguay in 1995 (see Goldmark, 1999). SE clients are provided with a discount voucher, redeemable against training; this lowers the cost to SEs, without reducing returns to providers. The theory is that by stimulating demand in the short term with a targeted subsidy, the benefits clients experience from the service will keep demand high after the subsidy ends – an approach used by many companies who offer lower prices for first-time customers.

It is assumed that the main reason that SEs are not using the service stems from a lack of information about its benefits (or even about its availability). The programmes also provide information to SEs about the discounted services. In Paraguay, the facilitator kept weekly statistics on which vouchers were redeemed, and publicized the results. Each provider was thus ranked, each week, so that all participants could see which training was the most popular.

Unlike FIT efforts, the focus of the Paraguay programme was not on the more informal end of the market for training. Vouchers were issued only to providers who had legal recognition as training institutes, that had taught SEs or SMEs for at least one year, and operated from formal premises with 'adequate' staff and materials. However, the leading institutes were typically 'small, private, for-profit organizations,' exactly the kind of provider our model (in Chapter 2) suggests is most effective for delivering services. The programme also targeted larger-scale entrepreneurs, the small to medium-scale enterprises as well as the micro- to small.

In Paraguay, the voucher reduced the cost of the course to the trainee by about US$20. The least expensive courses cost about $25, the most expensive about $70, so the voucher represented significant income for the institutes. Because vouchers were reimbursed only after the training course had been completed, providers were keen to satisfy their customers; so they stayed for the full course, enabling the trainer to redeem the voucher. Thus, the subsidy did not mask market signals in the way it might if it were delivered direct to providers. In Paraguay, training institutions that could not attract SEs became more competitive and developed products to match demand. The programme was publicized in the local papers and on the radio and this also benefited participating institutions. Finally, when their clients increased, so did their investments in their training businesses. Specifically, benefits of the programme included:

- An increased number of sectors were covered by courses. Part-time providers expanded their product range and invested in training materials. In line with SME needs, shortened courses with evening and weekend sessions were proposed, with simplified teaching methods and hands-on practice sessions.
- Possibly more SMEs trained. For the top three training institutes, a steady increase in the number of voucher and non-voucher clients was noted over the two years of the first phase of the programme, and over the nine months after the start of a second phase. Although the second phase was half as long as the first, it built on work done at the beginning; 19 287 vouchers were redeemed during phase one, and 29 264 during phase two.
- Lower prices. After initial investment costs raised prices of training, prices tended to fall as competition between providers grew. The subsidy also lost value.

The fall in prices was fortunate in the Paraguay case. In a market dominated by publicly funded providers this may not occur, due to lack of competition. In an imperfect market with few providers, voucher programmes may even drive prices up, as providers who do not face competition try to get customers to pay as much as possible (Hallberg, 1999).

It is still too early to determine the long-term impact of the programme on the training institutes after subsidies are withdrawn. It will be useful if future programmes try phasing out the vouchers earlier so that the impact can be monitored. It would also be interesting to see how important the role of advertising and provision of information about the training institutes is to the long-term sustainability of the training.

Despite the programme's efforts, market signals may nevertheless be distorted. The system might encourage people to try a more expensive service than they could otherwise afford. The information gained may not lead to ongoing investment, unless the service is good value without a subsidy.

What type of facilitator best administers voucher or other subsidy programmes?

The information available on the Paraguay voucher scheme does not go into great detail on exactly how the facilitator who screens the institutes, distributes the vouchers, monitors and controls the programme, and administers the reimbursement – is selected or created. In the first phase, a small team consisting of a government officer and two external consultants ran the programme. In the second phase, the programme was assigned to a government ministry in direct competition with private sector providers. The conflict of interest was problematic, but the scheme prevailed. The first team, more streamlined and without a conflict of interest, may have performed better. But they were subject to political pressures to channel subsidies in a given direction, which a stronger government actor can avoid.

After the success in Paraguay, the IDB may establish voucher programmes in nine other countries in Central and Latin America. A number of different types of facilitators, both public and private sector actors, will be used in different countries to test which type of facilitator might work best. An effective facilitator of a voucher scheme needs a range of skills: the administrative capacity to gather information and refer clients, distribute and redeem vouchers, and supervise and control the programme; financial capacity – so that funds can flow smoothly and the facilitator appears to own the programme; ability to stand up to political pressures; ability to network with SEs, policy makers and providers. These skills are available both within and outside government, but are not easy to find immediately in any given actor. Thus, facilitators may need to be recruited specifically to implement voucher programmes.

Matching grants

Matching grant schemes are the equivalent of vouchers for one-to-one consultancy services. They are usually organized on a 50:50 cost-sharing basis – but with a variety of different operational forms. Like voucher programmes, their aim is to assist SMEs and increase the information flow within the market. Matching grants are particularly common in World Bank-supported initiatives but many other donors and governments use them. To date, however, there has been little hard evidence produced to support the view that matching grants are a means to enhanced and sustainable consultancy markets. In fact, research in the UK, where a large programme was administered at a time when the market for consultancy services was in a growth period, concluded that the schemes had not made a significant impact.

Targeted subsidies

Both matching grant schemes and voucher programmes could potentially target SEs or SMEs that are particularly disadvantaged. For small-scale entrepreneurs who live in rural areas, however, voucher schemes may not be easy to administer equitably. Both types of interventions can enable specific target groups (in the short term) to take advantage of services that they could not otherwise afford, as an alternative to publicly financed services. The rationale for this type of intervention would be different; instead of aiming to remove constraints arising from a lack of information, it would be aiming to deliver subsidized services cost-effectively to marginalized groups.

Conclusion

The examples in this chapter and the previous one are just a sample of the ways in which the development of BDS markets can be supported. For the FIT programme, the role of the facilitator is central, and it is a multifaceted role. The facilitator knows the local SE sector, as heterogeneous and dispersed as it is, while being a player in the formal business sector. It knows the local economy very well. Straddling theses two worlds, and with the capacity to report, monitor and evaluate impact on behalf of the donors that support it, the facilitator scans the BDS markets, searching for ways in which commercial interests can bring services sustainably to SEs. FIT and ApproTEC have both developed facilitators that match these terms of reference. Although FIT works through facilitators that are commercial businesses, and ApproTEC is an NGO, both use donor funds to develop new service products that meet market demand. In its dealings with other businesses, ApproTEC operates as much like a commercial player as like an NGO.

The examples in these two chapters are in no way exhaustive. The sample sizes are too small to say definitively that these particular interventions should be replicated in other countries. However, they do provide some fresh ideas. Most of them point to the possibility of scale and sustainable delivery of services without too much dependency on public funds. They suggest that donors may have much to gain by moving out of a service provision perspective and into a service facilitation one. All of the interventions outlined are fairly new. It is too early to assess long-term impact. In the following chapter, however, we shall offer some suggestions on how impact might measured.

7. Managing and Measuring Impact

SEVERAL INDICATIONS HAVE ALREADY been presented that for-profit BDS providers can and do reach the poorest small-scale entrepreneurs; for example, Ugandan trainers noted that those who could not read or write appreciated their courses particularly. Similarly, those who could not speak a second language were also most appreciative of courses in their own language. This chapter will review in detail what the indicators of achievement should be, and the data that are already available in those areas.

Business development services potentially include any service that SEs invest in. The range and type of services are as varied as the range and type of businesses they support. Interventions to facilitate the development of new products, the effectiveness of providers, or the availability of services, are potentially equally varied, particularly if the dynamism of market forces can be tapped. Those who take an international perspective have an even greater challenge, as they must compare activities that occur in economies of widely differing size and complexity. At the same time, donors need to make investment decisions; facilitators need to know if they are using their resources wisely; governments, researchers and practitioners need to plan and execute research, activities, and long-term strategies. Some common basis of measurement is required.

Is willingness-to-pay a valid proxy measurement for impact?

When the FIT programme began in 1993 to develop sustainable and useful business development services for SEs, willingness-to-pay was considered the most important proxy indicator of both the positive impact of the service on the SE client, and of the potential for its sustainability. Evidence from the micro-finance movement, however, increasingly suggests that willingness-to-pay may not always be a good proxy indicator to measure impact.[29] Therefore, major efforts are under way in the field of small enterprise development to determine how best to assess the impact of both financial and business development services on the client, i.e. the micro- or small-scale entrepreneur and the enterprise he or she manages.

A common framework to measure project performance

Efforts to develop performance frameworks for BDS and for micro-finance programmes include research (funded by donors such as USAID and DFID), dissemination of findings and good practices, and consensus-building forums. For BDS specifically, the Donor Committee on Small

Enterprise Development has taken the lead in documenting and disseminating best practice in and developing guidelines for donors. Two international conferences were held to reach consensus on good practices in BDS, the first in Zimbabwe (1998), and the second in Brazil (1999). The case studies presented there formed the basis of part of the research undertaken to prepare this book. Now that progress has been made in defining what constitutes good practice, the goal is to develop a common framework to measure it.

In May and June 1999, with funding and technical support from the ILO and USAID, a five-week Virtual Conference on performance measurement for BDS programmes was held; it took as its starting point a Performance Measurement Framework drafted by Mary McVay, based on work by Development Alternatives Inc. (DAI) and the Small Enterprise Education and Promotion Network (SEEP). One hundred practitioners located in 27 countries and representing 20 organizations subscribed to the conference, while others were able to follow the discussion via the Internet. The goal was to determine a common, practical and valid framework for assessing the performance of BDS programmes that are targeted to micro-, small and medium enterprises.[30] The next steps for developing a performance framework are to prepare guidelines for case studies that apply it. The case studies will be presented at the next international Conference of the Donor Committee in Hanoi, Vietnam in April 2000, while USAID is sponsoring long-term field testing of the framework.

Meanwhile, what evidence of impact?

Signs that FIT facilitators have high potential for positive impact on BDS markets

Beyond the examples cited as evidence of impact of this new approach to BDS in Chapters 5 and 6, there are further signs that its effect is positive.

The staff of the FIT affiliate offices interact extensively with all stakeholders involved in the design and testing of a pilot service product. There is a great deal of impact information that is informally incorporated into short-term strategies and activities that the offices undertake. This is one way that the facilitators behave like a small entrepreneur, seeking feedback from as many sources as possible and learning by doing in a somewhat informal fashion.

In contrast to some development projects, where staff retain a stoical, philosophical attitude in the face of challenges, the FIT Programme is highly energized and optimistic. Commercial facilitators (like entrepreneurs) work round the clock, constantly thinking and discussing plans and strategies, learning and generating ideas.

Box 7.1: Tanzanian Travel Agent Finds a New Idea

As part of FIT activities, the manager approached a small-scale tour operator in Dar es Salaam to discuss the possibilities of business tours. Five tours were organized, with a partial subsidy from a project, that has now closed. The tour operator is continuing to organize tours for SEs without any subsidies; at the time of writing, a group of carpenters from Dar es Salaam has just purchased tour packages to attend an exhibition in Arusha, paying full costs. Meanwhile, the operator has also ordered ten beds from the carpenters – each offers the other a reasonable discount for their respective products. New business linkages, and new business development services, continue to grow. The tour operator thinks the private sector is the way to go. 'The project was providing the service (to SEs) but there was no real business relationship. I am working toward two-way business relationships with my clients.'

Evidence of the effectiveness of FIT service products

FIT's entrepreneurial approach proved useful for designing services that meet demand and can be replicated cost effectively. Many of the lessons learned are documented on the FIT CD-ROM or FIT Discussion Papers. Independent evaluations of exchange visits, which form the basis for the business tours, and a number of evaluations of User-Led Innovation (ULI), one of the training packages offered to small business trainers – were particularly positive.

Business tours are essentially improved versions of exchange visits to small and large enterprises. An independent evaluation found a wide range of benefits among visiting entrepreneurs; the most frequently cited included new production processes (including safer working practices), new product designs, new sources of spare parts, improved relations with customers and employees, and increased self-confidence (Hileman, 1995). 80 per cent achieved sales, 45 per cent higher, 58 per cent of the extra profits were spent on business expansion, the rest covered school fees, debts, marriage, and purchasing land or livestock. On average, each employed 2.5 additional staff.

Seven months after initiation of the ULI pilot, a range of innovative, agriculture-related equipment had been designed, and sales were strong; on average, each participating enterprise had sold new types of equipment worth $700. In addition, that key constraint to innovation – a lack of opportunity to communicate with customers – was effectively removed (Tanburn, 1996a).

The overall picture

Where the willingness-to-pay and anecdotal evidence indicated that FIT pilot activities merited further development, mini-evaluations generally found the services resulted in new products, new marketing techniques, improvements in production and overall changes in the entrepreneurs' approach to their customers. This was true for more than 50 per cent – usually between 70 and 90 per cent – of the participants, who also often reported new linkages (to suppliers, retailers, and peers). Evidence of increases in profits was sometimes available, but was difficult to find since clients did not keep financial records. An analysis of the GEMINI survey in Kenya found that net increases in sales were almost double the increases in employment (Parker, 1994). In other words, if employment goes up by certain percentage, sales are likely to go up by nearly twice that percentage. Employment increases may be a good proxy indicator for increases in sales.

Finally, an overall external evaluation of the FIT activities in Kenya interviewed 29 SEs who had participated in FIT pilots in four towns. Seventy-nine per cent reported that as a result of their participation they had acquired new product designs and technologies. Ninety per cent reported new customers, 72 per cent information on new markets, and 79 per cent new business contacts. Most also reported gaining new management techniques and improved self-confidence. Employment of full-time staff increased by 55 per cent. SEs who copied some aspects of the FIT pilot activities from their colleagues were also interviewed. They reported similar but lesser gains. Together with mini-evaluations conducted around six months or so after each pilot, FIT services proved effective enough to warrant further pilots to find sustainable means of delivering them. Under the latest FIT initiatives, with commercial facilitators working in collaboration with commercial private providers, there is every indication that services will remain in the market.

The state of play so far: how do we measure the development of markets for BDS?[31]

Measuring before an intervention begins – market research is the starting point

If the goal is to develop markets for services, the starting place is the existing market for the services. But instead of starting with a general survey of the market for a service, delineated by geography, SE target group, and the broad outlines of a service product, the local facilitator has the flexibility to start with an opportunity. The opportunity itself – a place where profit and development agendas potentially overlap – will determine a more narrowly defined service product, a location to test market it, and of the market segment SE customers targeted. The boundaries will be flexible, and commercial potential (not simply actual) will determine the area to be analysed.

73

Development agenda or profit agenda – different approaches to similar tasks

The donor or international facilitator holds the funds, but lacks extensive local knowledge. They must be thorough and accurate – qualities on which their own performances are measured internally. Local commercial facilitators and providers will be seeking the most economic route to achieve objectives, maximize profits and save time. Both must begin by defining the market in terms of:

- a geographical boundary – a town, region, city
- the small businesses targeted: this might be defined by size, whether the business is trying to survive or is in the process of expanding, but will probably be defined by sector. The local facilitator should be careful not to be more restrictive than is necessary, and to let the market determine who else the client could be.
- the service product: For development actors, product definitions should be made according to the actual activity – training, one-to-one consultancy, information supply, technology provision, etc. – and the specific subject of the BDS – financial management, technical skills, markets information, metal processing technologies, etc.

For local facilitators and commercially funded providers, the service product begins with a business idea based on a business opportunity. Facilitators will scan the market continuously in search of these opportunities. Once the idea has been defined far enough to be an opportunity, the facilitator conducts more detailed market research.

After defining the market, analysis can begin. Those with a purely development agenda require a detailed analysis of the existing market conditions. This is important not only to assess the results of interventions, but also because development agents, sheltered from risk, may not have the required local knowledge or entrepreneurial flair to make instinctive business decisions.

Data from both the supply and demand sides are useful: supply-side numbers, market cost structures including costs of entry (market contestability), performance data, SE current BDS purchasing patterns, and needs. The core question is: why isn't the market working as well as it could? What constraints are preventing it from achieving greater outreach, differentiation, competitiveness, quality, etc?

Commercial providers are seeking to offer a service that will make profits. For local facilitators, the question is what services that generate profits for large or small commercial providers or sponsors will also meet my development agenda? They may use other questions to find opportunities, but a good opportunity is something to investigate quickly. Research is simultaneous with, or leads straight into, test marketing. Local facilitators should have enough information and sufficient confidence in their own instincts to make a calculated assessment of risk and to assess the market by developing or testing a service product.

Measuring market development: core indicators

After the basic outlines of the market are established, indicators for assessing change in the market environment can be refined. The nature of the service product will determine the number and type of indicators most desired. For example, very few radio shows offer commercial information to SEs: each provider could be monitored. The many SE-style business trainers operating in rural areas, on the other hand, might require sampling. The following are the main priority indicators for assessing market development (core indicators). There should be sufficient data to permit 'before and after' comparisons. For each of the main indicators it should also be possible to set achievement targets, though they should be defined more flexibly than traditional achievement targets.

1. *Number of providers*: this provides insight into the competitiveness of the market and providers' perceptions of the opportunities presented by demand changes. There may be difficulties in defining 'provider' if they are selling other products in addition to the BDS in question; the definition could require a minimum proportion of turnover generated by the particular BDS.
2. *Size of the market*: this obviously tells us about aggregate trends in the overall volume of transactions in the market. It is most easily collected through the supply-side 'window'.[32] The final figure will not be precise, but it should be possible to gain an overall picture of market scale.
3. *Number of customers*: along with the financial size of the market, this indicator provides insight into market scale. A healthy market is clearly one that is growing. It should not be necessary to define 'customer' with respect to size of BDS purchase; if there's a transaction, there is a customer!
4. *Number (and proportion) of customers from priority groups*: this indicator provides insight into the degree to which the donors' resources are reaching the groups that they believe to be most important. It is likely to refer to business size and to gender.
5. *Number (and proportion) of multiple-user customers*: a proxy indicator for customer satisfaction and product quality. The development of a solid base of repeat customers indicates market maturity. For some types of BDS and providers – for example, assistance with writing a business plan – this may not be appropriate, but in many cases it will be useful.
6. *Percentage market penetration*: this follows directly from 1 above; provided that a base potential market and initial market coverage have been established, calculating market penetration is straightforward. This might also be measured according to coverage among priority groups.[33]
7. *General level and spread of prices*: related indicators that could be useful

in a number of ways. Lower prices might indicate a more competitive market; increased price differentiation may indicate greater quality differentiation; alternatively, reduced price spread might indicate greater knowledge among consumers.

8. *Costs per 'achievement'*: given the above set of data and provided that intervention costs are allocated properly, a range of indicators that relate costs to achievements can be developed. They might include cost per new provider; cost per new customer; and cost per unit increase in market size. If the last is known, the ratio of costs to change in value added among providers can be calculated with reasonable accuracy.

This set of eight indicators provides a solid basis for assessment. Using them to assess market development interventions should allow a transparent view of performance to emerge. For local facilitators and commercial providers, numbers 1-3 and 7 are the most important for test marketing an intervention. Donors, facilitators and providers collectively can measure the market for a specific service before and after intervention, monitor the implementation of the intervention, and obtain the core indicators.

There are some situations where core indicators may not be sufficient to give a clear picture of market development and where additional indicators relating both to customers and providers of BDS are necessary. A number of possibilities are outlined below.

Indicators that measure impact on customers

1. *Awareness (%) of available BDS*: borrowing from market research techniques, where brand recognition is an important early indicator of market development, a similar approach can be used here. This may be especially important where markets are underdeveloped. SE sample surveys or – for more qualitative data – focus groups could be used here.
2. *Reach (%)*: although similar to market penetration, here we are interested in the extent to which awareness is translated into purchasing decisions for BDS. In practical terms, this would require tracking SEs involved in surveys for 1 above.
3. *Satisfaction with services*: while the priority set of indicators acts as a proxy for satisfaction, this indicator goes one step further and seeks to quantify satisfaction levels and dimensions.
4. *Behaviour and performance*: again going one step further, these indicators – measurable only on a small sample basis – would seek to assess change in performance related directly to the purchase of BDS and track final 'bottom line' performance.

Further indicators that measure impact on providers

Indicators that measure impact on providers enable facilitators to measure their own impact on the market. Providers might be encouraged to monitor this information periodically as a management capacity-building exercise.

1. *Value-added*: providers are not always willing to disclose profit figures. Value-added – sales minus purchased inputs (equal approximately to profits plus wages) – may be a more practical indicator and also more useful in assessing economic impact.
2. *Awareness of customer needs*: this indicator implies that an evaluator will make an assessment of provider performance against a scale (determined by the evaluator) and track this over time. Quantitative scales designed to assess qualitative phenomena are not always practical; another method could be the use of focus groups that bring customers and providers together, to see what each says about the other and how closely opinions converge.
3. *Awareness of potential sources of new product ideas*: although useful, it is not clear how this indicator could be quantified. Quantifying supply-side networking may also be a useful way of assessing providers' broader strategic awareness.

Measurement of these indicators should provide a good basis for assessing market development and performance of interventions, including their outreach, impact, cost effectiveness and sustainability. While these indicators may leave a number of small gaps in the market profile, there is one very prominent weakness. No indicator directly addresses the market's ability to develop dynamically and to innovate. In practice, it is very hard to measure the value of product development. One could look to see if some of the conditions necessary for venture capitalists have emerged, if formal education encourages innovation, or if the legal frameworks are in place to protect licences and copyrights, and then simply monitor the new service products that appear.

Having identified a potential opportunity, the facilitator undertakes market research, to obtain answer to the following questions:

1. How is this service, or something similar to it, already operating in the selected market? Who and how many are the competitors?
2. What is the spread and range of prices? How much are these providers charging for the service or a closely related service? How are costs covered – in the customer's final price or in cash transactions? How much does the service cost for different market segments in different locations? This information will help to determine whether the intervention is creating any negative distortion.
3. What is the size of the market, the actual and potential number of customers? This is important information for facilitators to offer commercial partners. Facilitators will also want to tell donors how this market related to specific target groups.

4. How much money is changing hands for the existing service? How much more might move if the potential market was tapped? This information could help facilitators make sound investment decisions, as well as serve as a 'baseline' against which to measure progress.

This research, besides yielding the information a facilitator needs to introduce new services or improve existing ones, will be useful later to monitor the impact of the intervention. Since the indicators for facilitators clearly overlap with numbers 1 to 8 of the donor's indicators, care should be taken to avoid duplicating efforts and to ensure interaction between the two.

Methods for measuring impact cost efficiently

Main points to bear in mind

Techniques for measuring the impact of market interventions will depend largely on funds available, and the type of intervention undertaken. A number of general points should, however, be kept in mind when considering approaches to measurement:

1. *A proxy view (with all its imperfections)*: the core set of indicators is essentially based around the familiar 'profit-demand-impact' proxy,[34] where the assumption is made that successful providers can be used as a proxy measure for positive impacts on business. Other indicators seek to provide a more complete picture but there is, without apology, a considered leap of logic inherent in the approach. There are clearly arguments against this; it is known from the micro-finance experience that many and varied impacts can take place unnoticed beneath this indicator. Intervening organizations that need to know more about changes in MSE clients should supplement the core set of indicators with others focused on business change and performance.
2. *Getting providers to co-operate (why should they?)*: in practice, providers are in the best position to look at customers and examine their own performance. But why should they want to co-operate with efforts to assess how the market for BDS has developed?

    • First, because it is in their own interest to do so. Knowing how many clients one has, their identity, their response to products, etc. is useful information for their own operations. It is good business practice, let alone good BDS practice, and it is not an onerous burden.[35] If necessary, training or the development of simplified management tools could be facilitated to help them learn to measure their performance in relation to customers.

    • Second, because the sharing of information with facilitators and donors is made a condition of support. This may not be enforceable in practice but it may help create a habit of measurement.

3. *How to calculate cost–benefit ratio?*: provided that all the core priority indicators mentioned above are captured, it is possible to relate costs to achievements, as described. However, this does not allow the calculation of a net present value or return on investment. If this kind of cost–benefit analysis is deemed necessary, it would be practical only on a sample basis, ascertaining the kind of changes caused in SEs by purchase and use of BDS (value-added and employment, chiefly). Ideally, this should be checked against a control group. A number of questionnaires were developed by FIT that can be used to undertake this type of survey (Wesselink, 1995a, 1995b and FIT CD-ROM).

4. *Dealing with the big issues: attribution and displacement*: one key aspect of the rationale for market development interventions is that they reduce the scale of displacement. By not favouring one particular organization at the expense of others, we are deliberating trying to avoid the distorting impacts inherent in creating islands of high cost 'excellence' amid low-cost markets. Of course, the act of intervening always displaces something, and generally demand-side interventions (subsidizing the provider-SE transaction) are more distorting than those on the supply-side. Indeed, the displacement issue in market development is not so much about one provider being favoured against another but about the extent to which subsidies displace private sector activity per se.

Can the performance measurement indicators be simplified any further?

May the core set of indicators be further reduced to allow an even more *minimalist* approach to assessment? Of the eight priority indicators, only one – percentage market penetration – requires a full market survey to be calculated prior to the intervention. Should this prove too expensive or difficult, it could be cut. All the others are essentially calculated through the supply side, and their elimination would yield only slight economies. Initial market assessment concerns intervention design and implementation rather than performance measurement.

Regrettably, commercial providers and local facilitators without the support of an international facilitator may need to sacrifice accurate assessment for quick, flexible, and low-cost test marketing. Local facilitators need to keep to a minimum staff. They must be experienced in the commercial sector and may not have the relatively specialized skills to perform accurate impact assessment. A possible solution may be to outsource detailed impact evaluation, which could even give a more objective perspective. Where time and money are constraints, surveys can be replaced by focus groups that include both SE clients and SEs that are not clients. Focus groups can be followed up with carefully structured case studies.

Commercial market research, designed to be acceptable to actors in the commercial sector, is usually not as detailed as the core indicators. The depth of impact analysis required by donors, to reassure all critics that funds are used wisely to achieve social objectives, is likely to require the skills and input of an international facilitator. They can help local facilitators develop the tools they need to move good management practices toward good monitoring and evaluation practices.

Should anything else be measured?

The core indicators set out a basis of comparison between BDS interventions. Local facilitators, however, also undertake a broad but relatively superficial examination of the markets for many different services, in order to identify opportunities. They also test-market products and assess markets narrowly to gain enough information to plan the next action. In both cases, it is important to gather social and cultural data as they relate to the formation and operation of business linkages and networks. Networks will vary significantly, depend on the market segment one targets. Research in Bangladesh suggests that the services most valued by SEs are embedded in long-term relationships established between businesses and friends. Such relationships offer more than a single service product – they include market information, financing, and 'linkages' – the various deals that business people provide to each other to cement a relationship with tangible benefits. (Van Bussel, 1998).

International facilitators can help develop easy-to-use social science tools to measure, for example, the range and type of business linkages and networks operating in selected markets. Participatory Rural Appraisal tools can be applied to some types of data gathering. For example, Venn diagrams can illustrate relationships between and within businesses and business networks (see Figure 1.1). Information can be gathered quickly and consistently without expert input.

8. Conclusions

Myriad tasks for development agents – everything except service provision

AT THE LEVEL OF SERVICE (or 'assistance') provision there is a need to change the overall strategy for small enterprise development. There is much for the public sector to do at the macro-level, and governments can help enormously by establishing an enabling environment that favours all businesses, from micro- to multinational. They can ensure that policy, taxes, and regulations create a level playing field for everyone. They can allow more marginalized members of the business community to have an equal voice in policy making. They can regulate those businesses that operate unfairly or in violation of basic human rights or environmental and health and safety considerations.

Governments also can provide essential education and sustainable infrastructure – they also have the task of ensuring that legal and judicial systems are fair and effective. They can help to promote a business culture that is not divorced from, or considered in opposition to, social goals. They can supply market information, and they can accurately measure the economic performance of all aspects of the economy, including the 'invisible' SEs. But business development service provision, beyond basic education, certain types of information, and provision of public infrastructure, is not one of the areas that publicly funded actors should enter to any significant extent.

Paying for services empowers SEs

Public provision of services can keep commercial actors out of business. However, these commercial actors have the potential to be more sustainable, more customer-oriented, more affordable, and more embedded in local business networks, than publicly funded actors can ever can be. Public provision often fails to empower the recipients of services. SEs are productive actors who generate profits. They can influence markets with their purchases. They can become consumers who discriminate. They can demand, instead of merely being offered, services that meet their own needs.

Publicly funded provision weakens markets

Combining facilitation and service provision functions into one organization can create conflicts between development and profit agendas. Merging the two roles gives a high probability that the focus will diverge from the trends and opportunities available in the BDS marketplace to trends and

81

opportunities to access public funds. Service provision with public financing can create subsidies that cause unfair competition, and may discourage local investment and local initiative.

Let the market be the guide

With SEs encompassing so many and such varied types of businesses, designing a programme of interventions can be bewildering. Limiting interventions to small, discrete, windows of opportunity identified by a local BDS facilitator, takes the burden off donors and international facilitators who want to provide something for everyone, or support those with the highest growth potential, or those who are most disadvantaged. It means that interventions can be sensitive to differences in culture, and, if FIT-style facilitators are used, the financial scale can match the prices operating in a specific place.

Markets can ease the burden of development agents

If the private sector is allowed to meet market demand, wherever it may be, and take small steps to improve the technology, information flow, or development of new service products, the task of donors and international facilitators is much reduced. They need not design something for everyone: the market can take care of much of that. They do not have to focus on SEs with the highest growth potential, for these will no doubt be the SEs that commercial providers will try to target first. They may want to direct subsidies toward particularly disadvantaged SEs, possibly following the model set up in the Paraguay voucher scheme. But subsidies need to be monitored carefully to ensure they do not distort the market too much, and achieve their intended objectives.

The best hope for sustainability and scale requires a new perspective

Developing markets for BDS, whether increasing and enhancing the supply, or stimulating demand, or some well-matched combination of the two, offers a great deal of potential. If the interventions are done well, there is every hope that new or improved services will remain in the market for as long as they are useful. But a major shift in approach is required to achieve this. Development agents need to recognize the importance of local facilitators and the necessity of for-profit, SE-funded, providers. They need to understand that profit and development agendas can, and in the case of markets for BDS, should, overlap.

Non-profit facilitator providers will need to decide which way they want to go. By separating their provider and facilitator functions, the chances of impact and sustainability increase significantly. NGOs also need to realize that handouts do not empower people, particularly people who are learning to operate or expand a small business.

The way forward

The task of developing markets for business development services is very young. Research is required to develop a better understanding of how SEs use services at present, particularly the informal services that may not be immediately visible. There may be other types of for-profit, local providers that have so far not been noticed by development actors, as was the case with small-scale trainers. Once these providers are identified, it will be possible to answer the question of how to support them. What kind of support works best to facilitate these providers, without creating any dependency or negative distortion?

The question of how to measure market development has benefited from input from the world's SED experts, and preliminary indicators are ready. Now the indicators will have to be tested, to see if they are as practical and useful as hoped. More research into the development of BDS markets, and the impact of BDS on SEs generally, is required.

There is still little understanding of ways in which demand may be stimulated. Evidence of the effectiveness of matching grants and voucher schemes is still accumulating, and the final verdict may be out within one or two years. Meanwhile, what other possibilities are there for stimulating demand? Progress in defining good practice suggests that it may not be long before there is a clearer picture of how to develop, monitor, and measure markets for BDS. Even the smallest businesses are rapidly gaining access to telecommunications. Radio has already penetrated almost every corner of the world. Telephones, faxes and e-mail enable the global economy to encompass the most far-flung market players. The dialogue that is taking place among development practitioners on how to stimulate and support SED may soon be dominated by the voices of SEs and commercial providers themselves.

Notes

Chapter 1

1. The term 'small enterprise' is used throughout, to indicate micro-, small, and medium enterprises, in line with the working definition adopted by the Committee of Donor Agencies for SED.
2. Riddle: 1991 cited in *Business Services in Vietnam*, Service-Growth Consultants, Inc. and Thien Ngan (Galaxy):1998.
3. Collaboration under the FIT 'banner' was launched in 1991 between the ILO and the Dutch NGO Tool (now no longer in operation). The Government of the Netherlands has funded the initiative from its inception. The experiences outlined in this book refer particularly to the period 1997-1999; during that time, the programme expanded with funding from other agencies, including the Government of Austria, UNDP and the European Union.
4. With thanks to Kris Hallberg, World Bank.
5. FIT Steering Committee, 1993.
6. Botswana, Kenya, Malawi, Swaziland and Zimbabwe.
7. Klaus Schwab, convenor of the World Economic Forum at Davos, 1998, quoted in *Decent Work*, report of the Director General of the ILO, 87th session of the International Labour Conference, 1999, p.2.
8. This work supplements the material available on the CD-ROM produced for FIT by TOOL. Since the CD-ROM was produced in late 1997 the programme has intensified its focus on commercial service delivery.

Chapter 2

9. The arrows should not necessarily be taken literally to indicate funds paid directly by SEs. Income may be derived indirectly, as in the case of those who profit from establishing linkages, e.g. those who sell advertising services to large-scale industry to target the SE market, etc.

Chapter 3

10. Research in Latin America found that many establishments had high recurrent costs 'left over from decades of working with donor or government resources.' (Goldmark, 1999)

Chapter 4

11. For more information in general on the early years of the programme, see the FIT CD-ROM.
12. FIT's collaborators were generally NGOs but also for-profit providers who rely mostly on donor and government income.
13. Market surveys used fall somewhere between social science and market research in terms of time required, geographical range, and depth of analysis.
14. A study by Clifton Barton and Marshall Bear demonstrates just how effectively the commercial sector has responded to the need of small business people to use information technology to reduce transaction costs and expand their networks in the Philippines (Barton and Bear, 1999).
15. The analysis is based on the experience of FIT Uganda.

Chapter 5

16. The idea for the paper also built on efforts in Kenya to set up a similar news-paper. At the time of writing, FIT Resources in Kenya hopes to launch a similar venture very soon.
17. USAID and NORAD fund the programme.
18. To operate as a commercial player, one needs a steady cash flow and the ability to make quick decisions to use funds. Donor funding, even on a short-term contractual basis, almost inevitably presents obstacles to both.
19. In the five months that Tradeways Tours operated, a number of business tours were developed and marketed, and 28 SEs purchased tours, while another 19 business people purchased information to organize the tours themselves.
20. The Micro- and Small Enterprise Policy Unit of the Ugandan Ministry of Planning have subcontracted FIT Uganda, with the funding from the International Development Research Centre (IDRC), to conduct this work.
21. See Havers, 1998, for more details on ApproTEC's strategy and results.
22. ApproTEC does plan to scale up distribution, but plans to increase production, devolve customer support services to retailers, or structure the project like a commercial franchise were not evident from the literature reviewed.
23. The pilot phase ended in August 1998 but the project continues at the time of writing.
24. See Bangasser, 1996 pp.8-14 for an explanation of the differences between franchising and other commercial partnerships such as subcontracting and licensing. Also see Annexe 1 for two case studies of commercial franchises that have helped small business develop in Singapore (grocery stores) and Costa Rica (association of guesthouses).
25. See Tanburn, 1999, for more details of private sector training in Uganda, Tanzania, and Zimbabwe.

Chapter 6

26. For surveys of formal private sector training institutes, and a sample of the informal training institutes, see Bennell, 1997 for Zimbabwe and Bennell et. al 1998 for Tanzania.
27. Details about RMA and ULI can be found in Chapter 3. Grassroots Management Training was produced by the ILO SSMECA Project. It is a general business management course designed for non-literate business people.
28. FIT Uganda offered to pay 50 per cent of the client's fees for the first six months of training offered.

Chapter 7

29. Willingness-to-pay may be a more telling indicator for BDS than for credit. Cash is much more fungible than services. By deciding to invest time and money in a particular service an SE has already made a series of decisions that are structured around the future of the business. A decision to take a loan guaranteed by a group of peers is only a decision to take a loan. How to invest the money is a very complex and highly charged decision that is not necessarily based on an analysis of the optimal investment for the business. Almost any person connected to the borrower can try to stake a claim on the funds.
30. One of the moderators of the Virtual Conference, Alan Gibson of the Springfield Centre has summarized the results for measuring the development of markets for BDS, which are outlined (or quoted extensively) in this

chapter. The contributions to the Virtual Conference can be viewed at www.bellanet.org/sed/performance

31. Much of what follows in closely based on Gibson: 1999, with the addition of the local BDS facilitator's perspective.
32. Jim Tomecko of GTZ Laos in the virtual conference provided details of these approaches.
33. The Paraguay voucher scheme, for example, aims to increase penetration from 2% to 10% in three years.
34. A term coined by Rob Hitchins of the Springfield Centre in working with Swisscontact on a benchmarking guide for its business centre interventions.
35. For providers that operate informally, the imposition of management information systems may require investments in skills and technologies that do not offer any significant return on investments of time or money. Unless and until the provider is aiming for a more sophisticated market, informal management from memory may be perfectly adequate. There is no need to count customers, for example, if you know all their faces. In these cases, the facilitator needs to monitor provider performance for its own purposes, and will look for creative ways to monitor that benefit without burdening the provider.

References and Bibliography

Amenuvor, B. (1998) 'Impact Monitoring of FIT Activities in Ghana, 1994-1998' FIT Working Documents, FIT Programme, Ghana

Anderson G., (1998b), *FIT Uganda Ltd. Business Plan September 1998 – August 2001*

Bangasser P.E., (1996), *Franchising as an 'integrating' approach to the informal sector: some preliminary ideas*, ILO Geneva

Barton, Clifton and Marshall Bear (1999) 'Information and Communications Technologies: Are They the Key to Viable Business Development Services for Micro and Small Enterprises?' USAID, Washington DC.

Barton, Clifton (1997), 'Microenterprise Business Development Services: Defining Institutional Options and Indicators of Performance,' USAID, Washington DC.

Bennell P. *et al.*, (1998), 'Vocational education and training (VET) in Tanzania in the context of economic reform' DFID, Nairobi

Bennell P., (1997), 'Survey of private vocational training institutions in Botswana' DFID.

Coopers and Lybrand, (1998), *Zimbabwe: A nation-wide survey of MSEs*, Final Report for USAID

FIT Programme, – *Facilitating Enterprise Visits as a business opportunity: The FIT manual*, ILO Geneva

FIT Uganda Ltd., (1999), *A survey evaluating the demand and impact of training of trainers courses applicants for the grassroots management training course-Uganda*, unpublished by Kintu M.J.R., Kampala

FIT Zimbabwe (Pvt.) Ltd., (1998), 'A directory of small scale private trainers and training businesses in Zimbabwe' unpublished

Gibb, Alan, (1999), 'Strategies for NGO Development: combining sustainable outcomes with sustainable organisations, A model for development from South Africa)', presented the International Conference for Building a Modern and Effective Development Services Industry for Small Enterprises, Rio de Janiero, Brazil.

Gibb, Alan (1993), 'Key factors in the design of policy support for the small and medium enterprise (SME) development process: an overview,' *Entrepreneurship and Regional Development*, No. 5, p 1-24

Gibb, Alan, and George Manu, (1990), 'The Design of Extension and Related Support Services for Small-Scale Enterprise Development,' *International Small Business Journal*, Vol 8, No. 3 p.10-23.

Gibson, Alan, (1999), *Market development in BDS: where we are and how to go further*, unpublished, ILO Geneva

Grierson, John, Mead D.C. and Kakora E, March 1999, 'Business linkages in Zimbabwe: the Manicaland Business Linkages Project,' presented at the International Conference for Building a Modern and Effective

Development Services Industry for Small Enterprises, Rio de Janiero, Brazil

Goldmark, Lara (1996), 'Business Development Services: A Framework for Analysis', IADB Washington DC.

Goldmark, Lara, (1999), 'The Paraguay Voucher Scheme', presented at the International Conference for Building a Modern and Effective Development Services Industry for Small Enterprises, Rio de Janiero, Brazil

Goldmark, Lara (1998), 'Sorting Out The Truth: The Financial Viability of Business Development Services,' A paper presented at the Workshop on Business Development Services, Harare

Hallberg, Kristine, (1999), 'Small and Medium scale enterprises: A framework for intervention', The World Bank, Washington (Unpublished Paper)

Harper, Malcom and Gerry Finnegan (1998), *Value for Money? The Impact of Small Enterprise Development*, ILO Geneva.

Havers, Mark (1998), 'ApproTEC Kenya: Developing technology-based business opportunities'. Paper presented at the Harare Conference of the Donor Committee for SED on behalf of DFID (also available on the ILO web site, www.ilo.org, search for 'Donor Committee')

Hileman, Milena (1995), An Evaluation of the FIT/Pride Africa Exchange Visit Pilot, ILO, Geneva.

Hitchins, Rob (1999), 'Assessing the Experience of Swisscontact's Business Centre Approach in Latin America and Asia'. Swisscontact, Switzerland.

Kennedy, Richard, with Philippe Scholtes and Casper Sonesson (1999), 'The operation of three Romanian Business Centres'. Paper presented at the Rio Conference of the Donor Committee for SED by UNIDO and UNDP (also available on the ILO web site, www.ilo.org, search for 'Donor Committee')

Levitsky, Jacob (2000), *Business Development Services: A review of international experience,* Intermediate Technology Publications, London.

Mbeine E. and Anderson, G., August (1998), 'Sustainable training of MSEs through grassroots training businesses' A paper presented at the Workshop on Business Development Services, Harare

Masbayi M., (1999), 'A rapid appraisal of private sector trainers in and around Nairobi,' unpublished, FIT Resources Ltd., Nairobi

Mathuva, Joseph, (1998), 'Local Monitoring of FIT Activities in Kenya,' available on the FIT CD-ROM, FIT Resources Ltd., Nairobi

McCormick, Dorothy and P. Pedersen (ed.) (1996), *Small Enterprises: Flexibility and Networking in An African Context*, Longhorn, Nairobi

McVay M., BDS (1999), Performance Measurement Framework, presented at the conference on building a modern and effective development service industry for SSE 2-3 March 1999, Rio

McVay, Mary (1999) 'Virtual Conference on BDS Performance Measurement: Conference Proceedings,' Donor Committee on Small Enterprise Development and USAID office of Microenterprise Development, Washington, D.C.

Mead, Donald (1994), 'The contribution of small enterprises to employment growth in southern and eastern Africa', *World Development,* Vol.22, No. 12.

Mead, Donald and Carl Liedholm,(1998), 'The Dynamics of Micro and